THE GURKHAS

NIRALA SERIES

THE GURKHAS

Born on April 16, 1952, at Sallyan, Rapti Zone, KAMAL RAJ SINGH RATHAUR is Nepal's outstanding historian. He was educated at Tribhuvan University where he received the prestigious *Mahendra Vidya Bhusan.* Since then Rathaur has travelled widely and published his works in Nepal and abroad. He has lectured on the Nepalese history at different campuses of Nepal. In 1984 he visited RIMC, Dehradun to attend an attachment course sponsored by the Royal Nepalese Army Headquarters. In addition to this, he has participated in various nationally acknowledged research projects conducted by institutions such as CNAS (T.U.), IOHS (T.U.), and *Anchal Sikeshya Samiti.* Since 1984, Rathaur is associated with the military campus, Birendra Sainik Awasiya Mahavidyalya, Bhakatpur, Nepal, where at present he is working as the Principal.

He has also recently received Education Day Award. Currently he is working on the military History of Nepal for a doctoral degree from the Tribhuvan University.

NIRALA SERIES

THE GURKHAS

A History of the Recruitment in the British Indian Army

Kamal Raj Singh Rathaur

Nirala

Nirala Publications
G.P.O. Box 7004
Daryaganj, New Delhi-110002
niralabooks@yahoo.co.in
niralapublications.com

First Edition 1987
Second Edition 1995
Third Edition 2000

Cover Design & Illustration : Nandita Chaterjee

ISBN 81-85693-85-4

Distributed in Nepal by
White Lotus Book Shop,
Hanumansthan, Kupondole,
Kathmandu, Nepal

Printed at
H.S. Offset Printers
New Delhi-110002

Acknowledgments

Gratitude is expressed to the authorities of Foreign Ministry, HMG, Kaisher Library. T.U. Central Library, Royal Nepalese Army Headquarters for help and co-operation.

I am thankful to Major Chandru Rai, Captain Bhog Bhadur Gurung (of the British Gurkha), Bijendra Thapa and Manohar Gurung for providing rare materials related to this study.

I am also grateful to my wife, Mridu, for inspiration.

Abbreviations

B.S.	Bikram Sambat.
N.A.I.	National Archives of India.
R.N.A.H.	Royal Nepalese Army Head-quarters.
T.U.	Tribhuvan University.

Contents

Acknowledgments IX

Abbreviations X

Chapter One
PLATFORM
Probing the cause 21-31

Chapter Two
DIGNITY
Recruitment with admiration (1814-16) 32-41

Chapter Three
SMUGGLING
Recruitment with unfair, operations (1817-1857) 42-51

Chapter Four
REBUFFS
The British vital need and the Nepalese positive discouragement (1857-1884) 52-70

Chapter Five
PRESSURE
Recruitment under pressures (1885-1891) 71-83

Chapter Six
INTRODUCTION
The period of mutual accomodation
(1891-1914) 84-91

Chapter Seven
SURRENDER
Supply of recruits during the two
World Wars. 92-106

Chapter Eight
MYTH
Partition of the Brigade and after 107-110

Appendices 111-120

Selected Bibliography 121-124

The Almighty created in the Gurkha an ideal infantryman, indeed an ideal Rifleman, brave, tough, patient, adaptable, skilled in fieldcraft, intensely proud of his military record and unswerving loyality. Add to this his honesty in word and deed, his parade perfection and his unquenchable cheerfulness, then service with Gurkhas is for any soldier an immense satisfaction.

-Field Marshal Lord Slim

for all those
who inspired me to write this book

THE GURKHAS

The Gurkhas aiming a target.

The Gurkhas launch an awe inspiring khukri charge.

Gurkha Vc's along with Queen Elizabeth II of England.

Platform

CHAPTER ONE

"All the troops in the service of Nepaul with the exception of those granted to the personal honour of the kajees, Ummar Sing and Runjore Sing, will be at liberty to enter into the service of the British Government, if it is agreeable to themselves and the British Government accepts their services, and those who are not employed will be maintained on a specific allowance by the British Government till peace is concluded between the two states."[1]

The above quoted article extracted from the convention signed between the Nepalese Commander General Amar Şingh Thapa and the British General David Ochterlony soon after the capitulation of the fort of Malaun during the Anglo-Gurkha War (1814-1816) raises a sizzling paradox in my mind. The extract seems central to the issue of Gurkha recruitment in the British Indian Army. Why would one want to recruit the soldiers of the opponent troops? Before making an attempt of a dialectical analysis of this acute situation, let me draw attention towards one important letter dated 11th June 1815 from Secretary of the Government of India to Edward Gardner, Comissioner of Kumaon, for the formation of provincial troops of the Gurkhas:

".....the Governor General is pleased to authorise you to entertain as provincial troops for services in the Hills a proportion of Gorkhas, or Nepalese, especially such as have families resident in Kumaun and Garhwal, with regard to the number to be admitted into our service, you will please consult the commanding officers in Kumaun, by whose opinion jointly with your own the decision must be guided".[2]

In order to examine what lies behind this peculiar British interest in the recruitment of the Gurkhas, we have to study the major historical forces that made the British take this momentous decision.

Despite the constantly fluctuating nature of Indo-Nepalese relationships, a brisk commercial intercourse flourished between the Indian plains – namely Bihar, Bengal and Oudh – and the hills of Nepal. With the ascendency of the East India Company in Bengal after the Battle of Plassey in 1757 A.D., this intercourse was inherited by the British. Lured by the fact that Nepal was rich in gold, the East India Company made efforts of furthering the business transactions between the two. Before this, there was no direct relation between Nepal and the East India Company. Since the fundamental interest of the Company's commercial policies was to find out new sources of bullion, i.e. gold and silver, to pay for their imports of tea, silk etc. from their trade imbalance at Canton, the British sent English merchandise to the bordering districts from where the Company could extend its influences towards Nepal and beyond.[3]

The hitherto observed commercial intercourse between Nepal and the Indian states was disturbed by the rise of the Gurkha power. The man behind this upsurge was Prithvi Narayan Shah, the ruler of the small kingdom of Gorkha who had towards the end of eighteenth century lunched a campaign of unification. His seize of the valley of Kathmandu and new economic policies forced Jaya Prakash Malla, the ruler of Kathmandu, to solicit British help.[4] The decision formulated by the Select Committee to offer military help to Jaya Prakash Malla was communicated to the Home Government on 25th September 1767 in the following words;

> ".....for many years an advantageous trade has been carried on between the province of Bihar and the rich country of Nepal, by which a considerable quantity of gold, and many other valuable commodities were imported. The Rajah now dispossessed of the country, and shut up in his capital by the Rajah of Gorkha, the usual channel of commerce has been obstructed, and these provinces are deprived of the benefits arising from the intercourse, at a period when a decline of trade and scarcity of specie render it of greatest importance that every spring of industry should flow freely and without interruption".[5]

The Select Committee, aspiring to revive Indo-Nepalese trade relations by attempting to crush the gathering storm of Gurkha force in the valley, sent Captain Kinloch with a force of 2400 strong to assist Jaya Prakash Malla.[6] Captain Kinloch was defeated at the hands of the vigorous Gurkhas in August 1767 and was forced to retreat with heavy casualties.[7] Thus, the first British attempt of reviving trade relations with Nepal failed miserably.

This victory boosted the morale of the Gurkhas. As a result they were able to annex Kathmandu on 20th September and Patan on 6th October 1768.[8] A year later on 13th November 1769 Bhaktapur too was annexed. Having attained his dominion over the valley of Kathmandu, Prithvi Narayan Shah followed the policy of exclusion and expulsion of foreigners with utter rigidness.[9] This resulted in the expulsion of capuchin missionaries and the Kashmiri merchants. Conceiving a foreign policy of unified Nepal, Prithvi Narayan Shah described the Nepalese position in these remarkable words;

> "The kingdom is like a Yam between two boulders. Maintain friendly relations with the Emperor of China. Great friendship should also be maintained with the Emperor beyond the southern seas (the British) but he is very cunning. He has kept India suppressed and is entrenching himself in the plains. One day that army will come. Do not engage in offensive attacks, fighting should be done on a defensive basis. If it is found

> difficult to resist in the fight, then every means of persuation, tact and deceit should be employed".[10]

In this remarkable passage Prithvi Narayan Shah anticipated the Anglo-Gurkha war some forty years ahead. He clearly perceived the vital national interest of cultivating friendly relations with both China and India and stressed the need for being in a state of self-defence. This emerged out of his wisdom and his practical experience.[11] He was aware of the Company's evil design towards the little Indian states and had taken account of the miserable fates of those Indian states where the British first entered as traders and later established their political authority. Prithvi Narayan Shah, therefore, wanted to keep the British at arm's length.

The increasing bankruptcy of the East India Company in Bengal, the industrial revolution in England and the territorial expansion gave birth to a new British need. They were hunting new markets for their manufactures. This made the court of England more interested in the Company's trade expansion in the backward and less exploited hill areas to the north of India.[12] Hence, on February 11, 1768 an inquiry was made by the court of Directors in England to know if 'trade can be opened with Nepal and wheather cloths and other European commodities from thence to Tibet, Lahsa and the western part of China'.[13] In order to improve the commercial relations between India and Nepal, James Logan was sent to Nepal with the mission of convincing Prithvi Narayan Shah of the Company's benevolent attitude towards Nepal. He was to induce Prithvi Narayan Shah to open the old trade relation between the two countries.[14]

In 1775 Prithvi Narayan Shah was succeeded by Pratap Singh Shah. During his reign the Anglo-Nepalese relations did not improve. The successors of Prithvi Narayan Shah too adopted the policy of exclusion and expulsion. In reality what persisted was the stubborn British assumption that the trans-Himalayan trade through Nepal was possible. Fired by the desire of opening the trade through Nepal, the British kept searching for alternate routes. To fulfil this objective, Warren Hastings, the then Governor General of India, sent a British mission to Tibet under the headship of George Bogle by the way of Bhutan. In January 1784, again a British mission under the headship of Foxcroft was sent to Nepal with a present and the Governor General's letter to the King of Nepal.[15] This mission too like the previous ones crashed to the ground because it could not remove the suspision of the Nepalese rulers. Despite these misunderstandings, the concerned governments followed a policy of not being hostile to each other.

The foundation of modern Nepal laid down by Prithvi Narayan Shah was made strong by the efforts of Rajendra Laxmi and Bahadur Shah. In January 1790 under the command of Kaji Jagajit Pandey, Sardar Amar Singh Thapa, Captain Golaynia, Captain Rana Bir Khatri, Subba Jog Narayan Mall, Subba Foud Singh and Surbir Khatri, the Gurkhali troops crossed the river Kali and stormed into the region of Kumaon.[16] It was finally captured by the Gurkhali troops in February 1790.[17] Garhwal was also attacked and by an agreement was made a tax paying state to Nepal.

In 1792 the stream of Anglo-Nepalese relations took a significant turn. The chief cause behind this was the Nepal-Tibet war which started in 1788 and ended in 1789 with the conclusion of a treaty. However, hostilities were revived and on Tibet's request for military help, China sent a big force of 70,000 strong under a General Fu Kang-an.[18] This forced Nepal to court British help against Tibet and China. The Chief motive of the Gurkhali king was to ward off the Chinese through the British help. But the British played upon this golden opportunity and proposed for a commercial treaty. Bahadur Shah, then Regent, concluded this commercial treaty with the British on 1st March, 1972. The treaty regulated transit of goods at a stipulated rate of 2.33% *advolerem* invoice duty and arranged for the security of the treaty.[19]

Soon after this treaty was executed, the Gurkhas requested the British to provide armed aid against the Chinese threat. The Panchen Lama of Tibet too made an appeal to Lord Cornwallis seeking armed help against Nepal.[20] This put the British Governor General in a dilemma. Instead of giving armed help to either party, the British offered their mediation to both contending parties, hoping to bring about peace. To execute this, Captain William Kirkpatrick was ordered to proceed for Kathmandu. But before Kirkpatrick could reach Kathmandu Nepal sued for peace with China and a treaty was concluded between the two. Once this conflict was resolved, the Nepalese, no more enthusiastic about the British mission, declined to honour the treaty. The only valuable outcome of Kirkpatrick's mission was the preparation of an account of the kingdom of Nepal which he published in 1811.[21] In the meantime the treaty of 1792 between the British and Nepal remained a dead letter.

Having failed in improving the Anglo-Nepalese commercial relations and in settling the major border disputes, the British in 1795 once again sent another trade mission under the leadership of Maulvi Abdul Quadir.[22] This mission, like the earlier one, ended up in a failure. It could not induce the Nepal Durbar either to observe the commercial treaty of 1792 or to modify its policy of isolation.[23] Hence, from 1795 to 1800 Indo- Nepalese relations remained unchanged.

The statusquo in Indo-Nepal commercial relations was changed by an unexpected event which took place in 1800. That year, Rana Bahadur Shah fled to Banaras due to the internal political upheavals in Nepal. His exile gave the British the opportunity of manoeuvring a favourable political cum commercial position vis-a-vis Nepal.[24]

In the Nepal Durbar, Regent Queen Subarna Prabha, Kirtiman Singh Basnyat, Damodar Pandey and others wanted to confine Rana Bahadur Shah at Banaras even at the cost of concluding a peaceful treaty with the British. They were also afraid of the possibility that the British might help Rana Bahadur in restoration.[25] Hence, a negotiation between the Nepal Durbar and the East India Company was held to conclude a treaty of commercial alliance on October 26, 1801.[26]

As one of the provisions of this treaty, Captain Knox was appointed as the first British Resident at Kathmandu. Accompanied by Dr. Hamilton, he arrived at Kathmandu in April 1802.[27] But Queen Raj Rajeshwari returned to Kathmandu from Banaras and abrogated the 1801 treaty, forcing Captain Knox to leave Kathmandu on March 1803. In January 1804, the 1792 Treaty and the 1801 Treaty were formally dissolved by Lord Wellesley and Rana Bahadur Shah came back to Nepal.

On the pretext of the violation of the formal agreement by Garhwal, in 1803 the Gurkhali troops recaptured Garhwal and established the direct rule of Nepal.[28] In the meantime having defeated Sindhyia at the battle of Laswadi, the East India Company in November 1803, concluded the treaty of Surjeanyam Guon. Hence, the boundaries of the company extended up to the southern borders of Kumaon and Garhwal.[29] At this particular time Nepal and East India Company shared a common border in the western sector. Inspired by their overpowering enthusiasm the Gurkhali troops kept marching further west.

Having crossed the river Yamuna in the summer of 1806, the Gurkhali troops captured most of the petty states there. They crossed the river Sutlej and established their authority over the State of Katoch (Kangda). In the summer of 1809, they were attacked by Ranjeet Singh and were defeated. The Gurkhali troops evacuated Kangda and came back across the Sutlej river.[30] The assassination of Rana Bahadur Shah by his own brother Sher Bahadur Shah in 1806 marks the rise of Bhim Sen Thapa who was immediately made *Mukhtiyar*(Prime Minister)in Nepalese politics. The policies of Bhim Sen Thapa had considerable influence of Anglo Nepalese relations. With his drastic reforms in the military management, he became a naked dagger to the East India Company. Having trained his soldiers with the help of French experts, he built new barracks and cantoments and raised new army battalions. Thus, during the first phase of Bhim Sen Thapa's prime ministership the Anglo- Nepalese relations were reduced to the lowest ebb.

The Nepali policy of unifying the Himalyan States brought her in direct confrontation with the East India Company. War against Nepal was declared by the East India Company on Nov.1, 1814. Most of the foreign writers interpret the conflict as an outcome of the Nepalese aggressive attack on the English territories. Such a view is held by Pradyumna P. Karan and William M. Jenkins Jr.:

> Nepal's traditional suspicion in dealing with the British, and her determined effort to extend Nepal's frontier toward the south, brought Nepal and the British into conflict. Earlier forbearance and moderation on the part of the British Government were taken by the Nepalese as signs of weakness or, at least, of a reluctance to enter the rugged Himalayan area. Convinced of the impregnability of the Nepalese terrioty and of the invincibility of Gurkha troops, the Nepalese government adopted a policy of systematic encroachment upon British territories.[31]

Hence, the decisions to wage a war over the boundary disputes, they continue, was mainly due to the Nepalese confidence in the fighting spirit of the Gorkhalies. Let us have a look at an interesting fact pointed out by Leo E. Rose:

> The Kathmandu Durbar was anxious to avoid hostilities with the British. Orders were sent to Amar Singh to comply with the British demands and the Nepali detachments were withdrawn from the disputed areas.[32]

If one is to study the internal causes of the war objectively, the conclusion would be that both parties were equally responsible.

At this moment the Nepalese request for Chinese help was rejected. As the power of Manchus declined in the 19th century, China's policy towards the Himalayan states became increasingly cautious and defensive. China's utmost ambition became the maintenance of statusquo and that too merely by the means of diplomacy. The Amban's reply to Nepal reflects this typical Chinese attitude:

> "The Emperor is not concerned with whether or not you are associated with the British or whether or not you honour the British .... when you fight with the British, this happens out side our borders. The soldiers of the Emperor cannot go there".[33]

When Nepalese effort of finding allies in the war against the British failed, it had no option except to sign peace with the British. On March 7, 1816 a peace treaty was signed at Sugauli. In this treaty the districts of Garhwal and Kumaon and the Terai regions west of river Gandaki were handed over to the British. Nepal also agreed to receive a British resident in Kathmandu and to withdraw from Sikkim. Nepal was reduced to its present size by this treaty. The British captured the sites for the principal hill stations of India such as Simla, Mussorie, Almora, Rani Khet and Nainital. In the end of 1816, Lord Hastings modified the treaty and a portion of the Terai was restored to Nepal.[34]

Unlike the previous treaties of 1792 and 1801, the treaty of Sugauli had political overtones. Nepal was forced to the British arbitration in her differences with Sikkim. By Article 7 of this treaty, Nepal was obliged not to employ any European or American Nationals without the consent of the British Government.[35] This provision, to some extent, affected Nepal's sovereign status. It was during this war that the recruitment of the Gorkhalies into the British Indian Army could be traced.

References

1. Ramakant, *Indo-Nepalese Relations,* 1816 to 1877, New Delhi, S.Chand, 1968.
2. Nigel G. Woodyatt, *The Regimental History of the 3rd Queen Alex Andra's Own Gurkha Rifles,* London, Philip Allen & Co., Ltd., 1929, p.321.
3. H.A. Old Field, *Sketches from Nepal*, London, 1880, Vol. 1, p.273.
4. Ibid., pp. 267-268.
5. Campbel's Report-"*Foreign Political consultation*", Stiller type script, A type script of the real three of the Microfilm prescribed in the T.U. Library. p.4.
6. John Peamble, *The Invasion of Nepal,* London, 1971, p.55.
7. *Ibid*., p.55.
8. M.R. Pandey, "Angrej Haruke Nepal Prati Bhavana', 1768-1814, *Voice of History*, Vol.1 1974, p.11.
9. Sushila Tyagi, *Indo-Nepalese Relations,* (1858-1914). D.K. pub lishing House, Delhi 1974, p. 42.
10. Narahari Nath Yogi and Babu Ram Aachary (ed.) *Rastra Pita Shri Panch Bada Maharaja Prithvi Narayan Shah, Dev Ko Dibya Upadesh* (Divine Counsel of father of the nation His Majesty King Prithvi Narayan Shah Dev), Kathmandu Prithvi Jayanti Samaroha Samiti, 1951. pp. 15-16.
11. Yadu Nath Khanal, *Nepal Between India and China: An aspect of the evolving international balance in Asia, Centre for international* affairs, Harward University, Cambridge, Massachussets, February, 1971.p.7.
12. Sushila Tyagi, *op. cit*. p. 43.
13. *Ibid.*
14. K.C. Chaudhari, *Anglo-Nepalese Relations,* Calcutta, 1960, p.p. 37-38.
15. K.C. Chandari, *Op. Cit.*, p. 51.
16. D.R. Bhandari, *Nepal Ko Aitihasik Vivechana,* Krishna Kumari, Varanasi 1958, p.202.

17. Shiv Prasad Dabral "Charan" *Uttara Khanda Ka Itihas,* Part 5, Birgatha Prakashan Cadka, Garhwal 2030 B.S., p.71.
18. Sushila Tyagi, *Op. Cit.,* p.44.
19. Ramakant, *Indo-Nepalese Relations* 1816-1877, p.10.
20. Sushila Tyagi, *Op. Cit.*, p.45.
21. Leo E. Rose, *Nepal, Strategy for Survival,* Delhi, 1973, p. 71.
22. Sushila Tyagi, *Op. Cit.*, p.46.
23. *Ibid.*
24. *Ibid,* p.47.
25. M.R. Panday, *Op. Cit.,* p.12.
26. Sushila Tyagi, *Op. Cit.*, p.47
27. *Ibid.*
28. Shiva Prasad Dabral, *Op. Cit*.,p.36.
29. *Ibid,* p.p. 34-35.
30. *Ibid*, p.29.
31. Pradyumna P. Ksran and William M. Jennkims, Jr., *The Himalayan Kingdoms: Bhutan. Sikkim and Nepal.* D. Van Nostrand Company. Inc. Princeton, New Jersey, USA, 1963, p.84.
32. Leo, E. Rose, *Op. Cit*., p. 81.
33. Ramakant, *Nepal, China and India,* Abinav Publications, New Delhi, 1976, p.10.
34. G.D. Bhattacharjee, *India and Policies of Modern Nepal,* The Minerva Associates, Calcutta, 1970, p.17.
35. C.U. Aitchison, *A Collection of Tresties, Engagements and Sandas Relating to India and Neighbouring countries,* Vol. XIV, Central publishing Branch, New Delhi, 1929.

Dignity

CHAPTER TWO

The initial recruitment of the Gurkhas in the service of the Honourable East India Company is one of the most interesting aspects of the Anglo-Nepalese relations. By the end of the eighteenth century the Gurkha troops had reached the zenith of their power. They were moving towards the West Parallel to the territories which were under the protection of the East India Company. Once these two powers shared common borders, frontier disputes became frequent, as a result of which Lord Moira, the then Governor General of India, issued a declaration of war in November 1814. During this war the British Military officers closely witnessed the valour and bravery displayed by the Gurkha soldiers and were convinced of their brilliant fighting qualities. The exhibition of immense military powers gallantry, resolution and endurance by the Gurkhas during the siege of the fort of Kalunga all the more deepened the conviction of the British officers about their fighting skills. Referring to this siege, John Ship, then an ensign in the 87th Foot, paid tribute to the Gurkhas in these glowing words:

> I never saw more steadiness or bravery exhibited in my life. Run they would not, and of death they seemed to have no fear, though their comrades were falling thick around them, for we were so near that every shot told....[1]

Similarly captain Hearsay who too had fought in the Anglo-Gurkha War was one of the first to recommend the enlisting of Gurkhas into the Company's army. To quote him:

> "They are hardy, endure privations, and are very obedient, have not much of the distinction of caste, and are a neutral kind of Hindoo, eating in messes almost everything they meet with, except beef. Under our government they would make excellent soldiers".[2]

The height of this admiration for the Gurkhas can be discerned in a dispatch in which General David Ochterlony wrote, "the Company's sepoys could not be brought to match the Gurkhas". In the same dispatch he also recommended for the recruitment of the Gurkhas in the Army of the Honourable East India Company.[3] The British, who were convinced that "the Gurkhas were a great fighting people, who, if befriended, could be as much a source of strength for the Indian Government as they could be a cause of danger if alienated," thought it politically wise to recruit Gurkhas in large numbers. Hence, the "short, broad-chested, flat-faced, snub-nosed men with *khukri* in their waist-belt possessing dependable character, hardiness of life, love of enterprise, endurance in privation, tenacity to adversity and contempt for caste prejudices and rash temper, and warlike materials were considered desirable for the complete dominance of India. "The more Gurkhas we have, the safer we would be", was the watch word of the British.[4]

Thus during this war the British for the first time recognised the political overtones of recruiting the Gurkhas into the army of Honourable East India Company. During the first year of the war, General David Ochterlony requested the Company's Government in India to raise separate Gurkha Battalions.[5] Lord Moira, the then Governor General of Bengal, after a minute study, recommended this issue to the Directors of the Company for their approval. After the conformation of the Directors an order was issued on 24th April 1815. According to this order three Nussuree Gurkha Battalions were to be raised, which were to be designated as the first Nussuree, the second Nussuree and the Sirmoor Battalions.[6] Ochterlony was the first British officer who brought the concept of Gurkha recruitment into practice. Convinced of the iron will and fierce loyalty of the Gurkhas, he tried to form some army units from among the local inhabitants. The inhabitants of all the territories, west of the river Kali upto the river Sutlej recently conquered by the Gurkhali troops were considered 'Gurkhas' by the British. In reality they were not. They belonged to Kumaonis, Garhwalis and other such hill tribes. They resembled the Gurkhas only in physical appearance. Hence, in December 1814 out of those neighbouring hill tribes some irregular forces were raised by General Ochterlony. The result was that some of the local inhabitants who were serving as irregulars in the Gurkhali troops and had deserted Amar Singh Thapa joined the British ranks. But the crucial thing is that none of them were pure Gurkhas. But the British took them for the Gurkhas. Thus the soldiers of the first Gurkha unit in the Company's Army were infact non- Gurkhas i.e. Kumaonis, Garwalis etc. This was the unit which took a prominent part in defeating the Nepalese troops at Deothal on April 16, 1815.[7] The same unit helped David Ochterlony in his victory over Amar Singh Thapa at the fort of Malaun on May 15, 1815. This so called Gurkha unit was the nucleus of the first King George's Own Gurkha Rifles.[8]

In April 1815 when official order came for the formation of the three Nussuree Gorkha Battalions, the effort of recruitment at the Malaun front was operated by General David Ochterlony. With the surrender of Amar Singh Thapa on 15th May 1815, the war came to an end at the Malaun front. Soon after this, the Capitulation Act between the Nepalese Commander General Amar Singh Thapa and the British General David Ochterlony was signed. The fifth article of this act clearly states, "all the troops in the service of Nepaul ...... will be at liberty to enter into the service of the British Government".[9] This act facilitated the British Government in enlisting the Gurkhas for their newly proposed Gurkha Battalions. David O chterlony impressed by the valour of these warrior hillmen raised two Nussuree Gurkha Battalions at 'Subathu' from among the war-prisoners who surrendered at the fort of Malaun.[10] About 1600 soldiers accepted the British ranks.[11] In 1826 the two Nussuree Battalions were merged into one and thus became the premier regiment of the Gorkha Riflemen,[12] which later on became the First King George's Own Gurkha Rifles i.e. Malaun Regiment.

The evidence of the second major recruitment for the third Gurkha Battalion that took place at the Sirmoor front can be traced in an interesting incident. During the Anglo-Gurkha War the fort of Jaithak which was under the command of Ranjor Singh Thapa remaind the luring target of the British forces. The British forces under Major Ludlow and Major William Richards attacked the fort of Jaithak twice on December 26, 1814, but without success.[13] In the meantime Amar Singh Thapa sent a relief column of about 800 Gurkha soldiers under Rewanta Kaji, to Jaithak.[14] When the news of the dispatch of this relief column reached the British Camp, Frederick Young, who was the A.D.C. of General Gillespie, hastily collected 2000 recruits. On 20 February, 1815 Frederick Young surrounded the Nepalese relief column at Chanalgarh.[15] During the confrontation when the Gurkhas attacked on sight, the British irregular forces could not resist and fled for life. Frederick Young was left with a handful of other officers in the field. The Gurkhas surrounded him and asked why he did not flee with his men. To this Frederick Young replied that he had not come so far to run away. The Gurkhas were delighted by this reply.[16] Frederick Young, after his release was full of admiration for the

Gurkhas and later recruited them from the camp of the prisoners of war located in Dehradun and Sirmoor.[17] With the end of the Anglo-Gurkha War, this Battalion became Sirmoor Battalion. In this way, according to the order of the Company's Directors, the above mentioned three Gurkha units were raised.

But this was not the end of the recruitment drive which started during the Anglo-Gurkha War. Another target of the British forces during this war was Kumaon which had great strategic importance. The British wanted to sever links between Kathmandu and the Far Western territories of Nepal by capturing Kumaon. To attain this, the British did not have the sufficient regular forces. Hence, Edward Gardner, the commissioner of Kumaon, was authorised to raise some irregular forces. In response to this authorisation, Gardner enlisted the local hill men as irregulars. But he was not satisfied with this temporary arrangement. During the confrontations with the Gurkhali troops in Kumaon which were under the Command of Chautaria Bum Shah, Commissioner Gardner too was convinced of the fighting abilities of the Gurkhas. Hence, he also made the request for the permission of the Company's Government to raise a separate Gurkha Battalion in Kumaon. The British authorities in India gave due consideration to this request and in a letter dated 11 June, 1815, authorised him to enlist the Gurkhas as provincial troops for the service in the hills.[18] Accordingly a seperate Gurkha Battalion designated as Kumaon Battalion was raised by Sir R. Colquhoun. Later on, the same Battalion became the Third Queen Alexandra's Own Gurkha Rifles.[19] When war ended in the west 4650 Gurkha soldiers were already enlisted in the four Gurkha Battalions. Each Gurkha Battalion was to consist 8 Companies with 120 persons in each Company.

Jang Bahadur Rana, Prime Minister of Nepal

A moment of rest, World War II.

The British and Gurkha officers of 1/ist Gurkhas outside the battalion headquarters on the northern sector of the western Front in August 1915.

A Gurkha soldier in action.

A still from World War II.

References

1. Byron Farwell, *The Gurkha*. Penguin Books, Great Britain, 1985, p.30.

2. *Ibid*, p.32.

3. David Bolt, *Gurkhas,* London, p.59.

4. D.C. Boulger, *England and Russia in Central Asia,* London, 1879, p.65.

5. David Bolt, *Op. Cit.,* p.59.

6. Macdonald Macanlay, *History of the 4th Prince off Wales Own Gurkha Rifles (1857-1937)*, London, 1940, Vol.1, p.2.

7. *Ibid.*

8. *Ibid.*

10. P.Landon, *Nepal,* Vol. II. London, 1920. p.191.

11. Shiva Prasad Dabral, *Op. Cit.,* p. 418.

12. Donoven Jackson, *India Army,* London, 1940.

13. Shiv Prasad Dabral, *Op. Cit.,* p. 418.

14. *Ibid*

15. *Ibid*

16. David Bolt, *Op. Cit.,*p.p.59-60.

17. *Ibid* p.60.

18. Nigel G. Woodyatt, *The Regimental History of the 3rd Queen Alex Andra's Own Gurkha Rifles,* Philip Allen & Co., Ltd., 1929, p.321.

19. *Ibid.*, p.3.

Smuggling

CHAPTER THREE

The first drive of the Gurkha recruitment had already stopped with the end of the Anglo-Gurkha war. The court of Directors of the Honourable East India Company, ever preaching economy to its agents in India, were no longer interested in maintaining these Battalions. But the important factor that emerged almost immediately after raising of the battalions was the enthusiasm of the British officers, who were convinced of the martial qualities of Gurkhas, and wanted to test their worthiness in the British Indian Army. The Sirmoor Battalion, which took part during the third Anglo- Mahratta War of 1817-18, became the first of the Gurkha Battalions to see action under the British. But the first battle honour was won by the soldiers of both the Sirmoor and Nussuree battalions at the siege of Bhurtpore in 1825-26. In 1825 Baldeo Singh, ruler of Bhurtpore, died and his young son, Balwant Singh, ascended the throne. Within a few weeks, Doorjan Sal, a nephew of the late ruler, staged an uprising which result ed in the imprisonment of the young ruler. The British Government who had already recognised the sovereignty of the young ruler considered this as an open defiance. The move for restoration was initiated and a force of 21,000 man and 100 guns under the command of Lord Combermere was dispatched to siege the fort of Bhurtpore. The Sirmoor and Nussuree Gurkha battalions actively participated in this battle displaying a spirit of unswerving loyalty to their new masters. The fierce battle fought in January 1826 finally resulted into the imprisonment of Doorjan Sal and the restoration of Balwant Singh to his throne. The last operation was ably assisted by Sirmoor Battalion and this became their first battle honour. For this, Divisional Commander, Major General Nicolls highly praised them.[1] It was at the end of this six-week siege that the Gurkhas on the one hand complimented the English troops by saying "they (the British) were very nearly the equal to us", the British on the other hand got right opportunity to test their worth. The British authorities in India thenceforth started to think seriously about the desirability of the Gurkha Battalions.

The two important men who played the key role in furthering the Gurkha recruitment in the British Indian Army were Sir Edward Pagets and Brain H. Hodgson. In 1825 Sir Edward Paget, the then Commander-in-Chief of the British Indian Army, proposed the augmentation of the strength in the Gurkha Battalions and the formation of the new ones by fresh recruitments. Mr. Gardner, the then resident at the court of Nepal, in turn was directed to report on the propriety of adopting this plan. He was also asked to shed light on the willingness and fitness of otherwise for general service of the Nepalese military tribes in the British Indian Army.[2] In a dispatch to the Indian Government, dated January 31, 1825, Mr. Gardner, having admitted that the Gurkhas were "brave and hardy race, tractible and orderly", described that no unit of Indian troops could be found superior to the Gurkhas. He also stressed the need of the Gurkhas who were trained in the British model to fill the British ranks. But no great number of Gurkhas, Gardner said, would prefer to come to serve the British even if it were free to them.[3] Hence, Mr. Gardner looked at the feasibility of this plan with some doubt for he believed that:

> Even on entering our service the Gurkhas would not separate themselves entirely from their native country, as they

> could not remove their families from Nepal and however faithfully they might conduct themselves on general ocassions, in event of any future rupture with Nepal, they possessed that feeling of patriotism which would induce the greater part of them to adhere decidedly to their national allegiance.[4]

A better plan, in the opinion of Mr.Gardner, would have been to negotiate with Nepal for the service of a portion of her organised troops as mercenaries. It would have also relieved Bhim Sen Thapa of the expense of maintainance of a large well drilled Army in a state of enforced idleness and restiveness. But nothing came out of this plan because the employment of separate bodies of foreign mercenaries were against the British military policy.

At this point Brain H. Hodgson, assistant Resident at Kathmandu, who had keenly observed the millitary tribes of Nepal proposed new and separate Gurkha Battalions. Edward Gardner's successor, Sir Herbert Maddick, too understood the undercurrents of Hodgson's pragmatic plans.[5] Sir Maddick was succeded by Hodgson as Resident to Nepal in 1833. Before he succeeded Meddick, Hodgson had submitted his report on military tribes of Nepal to Indian Government in October 1832,[6] in which he wrote;

> These highland soldiers, who dispatch their meal in half an hour and satisfy the ceremonial law by merely washing their hands and face and taking off their turbons before cooking, laugh at the para physical rigour of our sepahees, who must bathe from head to foot and make pooja, are they begin to dress their dinner, must set merely nacked in the coldest weather, and can not be in marching trim again in less then three hours, the best of the day. In war the former carry several days provisions on their backs the latter would deem such an act intolerably degrading, the former see in foreign service nothing but the prospect of gain and glory, the latter can discover in it nothing but pollution and peril from unclean men and terrible, wizards, goblins and evil spirits.
>
> In masses, the former have all that indomitable confidence each in all, which grows out of national integrity and success,

> the latter can have no idea of this sentiment in peril, better than all human bonds whatever.[7]

Hodgson compared the Gurkha to the Indian native soldiers and tried to prove that the former were superior to the latter in every respect. He calculated that there were about 30,000 Dhakre or unemployed warriors by annual Pajani system.[8] Hence, Hodgson strongly urged the British Indian Government to adopt the policy of drafting surplus soldiery of Nepal in the British Indian Army:

> ...I am well assured their service if obtained, would soon come to be most highly praised. In my humble opinion they are by far the best soldiers in India, and if they were made participates of our reknown in arms, I. consider that their gallant spirit and unadulterated military habits might be relied on for fidelity, and that our good and regular pay and noble pension establishment would serve to counterpoise the influence of nationality, especially in the Magars and Gurungs.[9].

Hodgson considered the immediate implementation of his plan as a fruitful measure of military policy in strengthening British grip over India.[10]

But the British Government did not give approval to Hodgson's plan, thinking that the hostile Anglo-Nepalese relations caused by the war of 1814-16 would hinder the recruitment of the best fighting materials of Nepal in the British ranks. But unruffled, during his ten years of residency (1833-1843), Hodgson continued his efforts of bringing the two powers together on the recruitment issue. In December 1843 Hodgson was succeeded by Major H.M. Lawrance.[11] Lawrance too, like Hodgson, recommended the Gurkhas for the British ranks. He proposed to make service conditions for the Gurkhas more attractive. He also asked the British Government to reserve 3/4 of the native commission for them. He further recommended that the popular and capable officers should be sent to Nepal for enlistment of the Gurkhas with the assistance of the Resident.[12] But before his recommendation could be realised, he retired in 1846.

The first Anglo-Sikh War of 1845-46 provided another opportunity for the Gurkhas to distinguish themselves. After the death of Ranjit Singh, Khalsa army of Sikhs in Punjab crossed the river Sutlej and invaded the British India. During his war Nusseree and Sirmoor Battalions fought in the battles of Aliwal and Sobraon. In the battle of Aliwal Gurkha, Havilder Badal Sing Thapa was given the Indian Order of Merit. At Sobraon, too, four Gurkha Soldiers won the Indian Order of Merit.[13] It was for the first time that the Gurkhas won some distinguished awards in the battle. General Sir Hugh Gough, in his after-action report on these battles, wrote:

> "I must pause in this narrative especially to notice the determined hardihood and bravery with which our two battalions of Goorkhas, the Sirmoor and Naseree, met the Sikh whenever they were opposed to them. Soldiers of small stature and indomitable spirit, they vied in ardent courage in the charge with the Grenadiers of our own nation and, armed with the short weapon of their mountains, were a terror to the Sikhs throughout great combat".[14]

In 1850 the whole of 66th Bengal Native infantry at fortress of Govindghur in Punjab got disbanded because of its mutinous behaviour over the question of some extra allowance. This infantry was replaced by the Nusseree Battalion with new designation of 66th or Gurkha Regiment, Bengal Native Infantry.[15] This was the first Gurkha Battalion which got the prestige of becoming the regular Gurkha Regiment.

Recruitment, for maintaining the existing three Gurkha Battalions, was not an easy job. Due to the lack of definite arrangements for the recruitment, the indirect means were the only alternative. In 1843 the British Government in India established a recruiting depot across the Nepal border. A recruiting agent was sent to Nepal to attain the required forces for the depot. But the agent was arrested by Nepalese authorities, and the ban on enlistment in the British Indian Army was widely publicised.[16]

The role of the Gurkhas was becoming crucial for the functioning of the British machinery in India. From British standpoint, thus, the persuasion of Nepalese Prime Minister Jang Bahadur was an inevitable necessity. In 1850, Lord Dalhousie, the then Governor General of India, thought of augmenting the strength of the Gurkha Battalions. This move of Governor General coincided with the visit of Jang Bahadur to England. The Nepalese Prime Minister assured that he would help the British in getting the Gurkha recruits.[17]

The moment the British got Jang Bahadur's assurance regarding the Gurkha recruitment, they instructed the British authorities at the court of Nepal to rush for recruits from Nepal. Major O. Brain, the commanding officer of Nusseree battalion in 1850, asked the British Resident Thoresby at the court of Nepal to influence Bam Bahadur, the then officiating Prime Minister in getting the recruits.[18] Outwardly, Bam Bahadur displayed a posture of co- operation and a British recruiting party arrived in November 1850. A notice asking the recruits to come was issued by the Nepalese government but when the thousands of Gurkha recruits came, the Nepalese Government prohibited them from going to Residency on the pretext that if they were allowed to go there, they would be forcibly enlisted.[19] Thus, indirectly the British attempt was thwarted.

Disappointed, when the recruiting party was about to leave for India, General Bam Bahadur again assured the co-operation, asking the British to select the recruits in his presence. Finally the recruits selected by the Prime Minister were sent to the Residency for final selection. Accordingly only fifty to sixty recruits could be selected. Twenty recruits out of those finally selected were found unfit and only thirty two were set free for India to join the Gurkha Battalions.[20] Hence, this British mission ended up in sheer waste of time and money. They continued getting Gurkha recruits *Sub rosa.*

When Jang Bahadur returned from England in 1851, the British Resident hoped for some substantial change in Nepal Durbar's attitude towards the recruitment issue. But the core of Jang Bahadur's foreign policy with the British was diplomatically contradictory. He isolated the British in those contexts in which he spoke aloud for a friendly co-operation. He nourished a very stiff nationalistic attitude towards the free movement of Europeans and their commercial intercourse. In 1854, Jang Bahadur, discouraging Nepalese recruits to join the British ranks, declared that he would not allow "a single Gurkha *Sipahee* in the British service to enter Nepal unless he had first taken discharge".[21]

The chief cause behind this discouraging policy was the ill- feeling and misunderstanding caused by great number of Nepalese criminals who had entered British services. Their return to Nepal, Jang Bahadur feared, might disrupt the normal life of Nepalese civilians. Secondly, Jang Bahadur did not allow the enlistment of Gurkhas in the British Indian Army because at that time the Europeans, too, were not allowed to serve the Nepalese Government. Lastly, Jang Bahadur was acutely conscious of the economic status of the Gurkhali troops. If he waved his objections, he knew, thousands of Gurkhas attracted by the superior advantages of pay, pension and other facilities, might desert Nepal to join the British ranks. In other words, Jang Bahadur did not want the British to mine the Gurkhali riches. Jang Bahadur thought that the liberal attitudes might deprive the Nepalese Government of sufficient human resources.

Moreover, Jang Bahadur and other Nepalese chiefs regarded the enlistment of the Gurkhas in the British

Indian Army as an act of humiliation. They considered the Gurkha recruitment a sinister and malvolent design, conceived to denude Nepal of its fighting population. It appeared to them an act against the Nepalese prestige. Though Jang Bahadur vehemently believed in the assumption that the Gurkha recruitment in the British Indian Army was suicidal for Nepal, he could not flatly refuse the British request because during his visit to England he had given them the word of assurance. Instead, he tried to sidetrack the recruitment issue by creating internal and indirect obstacles.

The then Resident to Nepal, Mr. Ramsay, attributed the stiff non- cooperative attitude of Nepal Durbar towards the British to numerous unfortunate factors. The first factor which inflamed the conflict between the two parties was the sense of superiority that a Nepalese soldier displayed at home. During his leave the Nepalese soldiers from the British Indian Army sang songs of the magnitude and the power of the British Empire. Secondly, in Mr. Ramsay's opinion, some stray events too caused the misunderstanding between Nepal Durbar and the British Indian Government. For example, on an occasion a Newar soldier from British Indian Army on his return to Nepal addressed himself as Jang Bahadur. To Jang Bahadur it appeared an act of humiliation. In another example in 1853 while Bam Bahadur visited Almora, an untouchable (a Damai) was appointed to attend his person by the commissinor of Kumaon. This caste factor too played a negative role and enraged the Nepal Durbar.[22] Mr. Ramsay's response to Jang Bahadur's stiff attitude seems extremely apt:

> My impressions are that we must expect fewer liberal measures from General Jang Bahadur than from any of his predecessors despite the intentions he proclaims, while he is travelling in our provinces.[23]

The British-Indian Government strongly remonstrated against the Nepalese attitude and requested Jang Bahadur to withdraw some of the restrictions imposed on the Nepalese subjects serving the British Army.

In response to the British remonstration, Jang Bahadur revised his attitude to some extent.[24] He agreed that the Gurkhas should come to Nepal in civil dress, not in British uniforms. They were also asked to behave like Nepalese subjects and were forbidden to visit Kathmandu and the neighbouring military stations. They were also asked to come with the valid passport from the Resident. Above these conditions, the soldiers working in the Indian Army were ordered not to enter Nepal through direct route of Sugauli. Although Jang Bahadur did not want to be a candid opponent to displease the British, his overall attitude always hindered the flourishment of the Gurkha Regiments in the British Indian Army. In 1856 Lord Dalhausie before leaving for India strongly recommended an enormous expansion of the Gurkha forces in the Indian Army.[25] In May 1857 when the Mutiny broke out in India, the British forces decided to raise some extra regiments.[26] To meet the requirements of the Mutiny the forces of extra regiment at Almora was channelised for a seperate regiment designated as the Fourth Gurkha Regiment. This Regiment which later became a regular Gurkha Regiment in 1861 was the last Regiment raised by the government of the East India Company. The exquisite fighting capacity displayed by the Gurkhas during the mutiny gave birth to a vigorous recruitment drive.

References

1. Christopher Chant, *Gurkha*, Blandford Press, Poole Dorset, England, 1985, p.25.

2. *Foreign political Consultation,* 23rd January 1835 No.50, Stiller typescript (*A Typescript of the real three of the Microfilm* preserved in T.U. Library. p.54).

3. *Ibid*., p.55.

4. *Ibid.*
5. W.W. Hunter, *Life of Brain Houghtson Hodgson, British Resident at the court of Nepal,* John Murray, London, 1896, p.107.
6. *Foreign Political Consultation,* Stiller Type Script, Op. Cit., p.56.
7. *Ibid.*, pp.56-57.
8. *Ibid.*, p.57.
9. *Ibid.*
10. W.W. Hunter, *Op. Cit.,* p.107.
11. Ramakant, *Indo-Nepalese Relations,* p.218.
12. H.Lawrence, *Essays on the Indian Army and Oudh,* p.230.
13. Byron Farwell, *Op. Cit.,* pp.38-39.
14. *Ibid.* p.39.
15. J.B.R. Nicholson, *The Gurkha Rifles,* Osprey Publishing Ltd., England, 1974, pp.8-9.
16. *Foreign Secret Consultations,* April 19, 1843, No.52.
17. *Foreign Political consultations,* August 11, 1854, No.11. (N.A.I.).
18. *Foreign political Consultations,* February 7, 1851, No.144. (N.A.I.).
19. *Ibid.*
20. *Ibid.*
21 *Foreign Political Consultations,* August 11, 1854, No.11. (N.A.I).
22. *Foreign Department Political,* July 1866, No.64. (N.A.I.).
23. *Foreign Political Consultations,* August 11, 1854. No.11-12, (N.A.I.).
24. *Foreign Political Consultations,* August 11, 1854, No. 12, (N.A.I.).
25. Sir. Francis Tuker, *Gorkhas, the story of the Gurkhas of Nepal,* Costable and Compay Ltd., Lodon, 1957. p. 121.
26. Macdonell and macauly. *Op. Cit.*, p.4.

Rebuffs

CHAPTER FOUR

The Indian Mutiny of 1857 is a significant event in the history of the British Indian Army.The Mutiny, which started in May 1857, spread over to the whole Bengal Army. But the Gurkha Battalions remained unaffected. At this crucial moment, when almost all the native troops joined the mutineers, the Gurkhas remained loyal to the British. Not only this, the Gurkhas also played a vital role in suppressing the Mutiny. As a mark of goodwill, the Government of Nepal also offered active support. As soon as the Mutiny began Nepal offered to send its regular troops to help the British. Under the Command of Nepalese Prime Minister Jang Bahadur, a contingent of 6000 soldiers marched into northern India and helped the British to recapture the important city of Lucknow. As a token of gratefulness the British Government returned a portion of Terai along the India's northern border to Nepal.

The Mutiny, which was a shattering experience for the British, necessiated the reassessment of the nature of the British rule in India. As a result of which on 1st September 1858 the administration of India was taken over from the Honourable East India Company by the British Crown. The change in administration also marked the change in the Indian Military Organisation. After the Mutiny the role of the Gurkhas in the British Indian Army had become more crucial. The British authorities in India were convinced of the fact that besides the European soldiers no soldiers in the Indian Army were more valued than the ever-gallant and hard- fighting Gurkhas. The worth of Gurkhas was now recognized and they were officially styled riflemen rather than sepoys.

Hence, the vital need of the British in the post-Mutiny era, was to augment the Gurkha Battalions. The Fifth Gurkha Battalion was raised in 1858 by Henry Ramsay, the then Commissioner of Kumaon from the Gurkhas in the Sikh Army at Abbottabad.[1] In addition to this a number of illegal recruiting teams were sent into Nepali hills to seek recruits for the then existing five Gurkha Battalions in the British Indian Army.[2] In order to augment the Gurkha strength in the Indian Army, in 1859, the Gurkha Battalions were exempted from the ban imposed upon the general recruiting for all native due to economic reasons.[3] The height of the British interest in the Gurkha recruitment can be clearly seen here.

During the reorganisation of the Indian Army in 1861, the British Government gave much more importance to the Gurkha Battalions. All the five Gurkha Battalions were reorganised on regular basis into the different Rifle-Regiments. In this reorganisation the Nusseree Battalion raised on April 24th 1815 and made the 66th Gurkha Regiments of Bengal Light Infantry in 1850 was reorganised into the First Gurkha Regiment; the Sirmoor Battalion raised on 24th April, 1815 was made the Second Gurkha Regiment; the Kumaon Battalion which was raised on June 11 1815, was designated as the Third Gurkha Regiment; the extra Gurkha Battalion which was raised in 1857 was made the Fourth Gurkha Regiment and the Hazara/Gurkha Battalion raised in 1858 was designated the Fifth Regiment. The charter issued by the British Indian Government in 1864 all the more helped in furthering the status of the Gurkha Regiments. The charter provided for the Gurkha Regiments to buy land for their permanent stations at Dharamsala (1st Gurkhas), Deharadun (2nd Gurkhas), Almora (3rd Gurkhas), Bakoh (4th Gurkhas), Abbottabad (5th Gurkhas)[4] This was the origin of the differ ent Gurkha colonies in these areas.

The vital interest of the British Government was not in keeping with the policies of Nepal Durbar. Nepalese authorities during this phase of history too exhibited a policy of positive discouragement in the context of the Gurkha recruitment. But the centrifugal British forces were diplomatically at work in bringing the favour of the Nepalese Government for the British, Overtly, though Jang Bahadur and Ranoudip displayed a pose of extreme generousity and helpfulness, in the heart of their hearts they suppressed the Gurkha recruitment. Whenever Jang Bahadur offered help to the British, be it the armed help during the Anglo-Sikha War (1848), and the Indian Mutiny (1857) or his diplomatic visits to England in the beginning of 1850, it was to earn British goodwill.

In a book called *Land of Gurkhas*[5] W.B. Northey has stated that in the troubled years of the Indian revolt i.e. 1857-58, Nepal not only recognised the existance of the Gurkha Regiments in the British Army but also assisted in the recruitment. But to me, Mr. Northey's hypothesis seems historically groundless because no fundamental change took place in the attitude of Jang Bahadur. In August 1 1858 Jang Bahadur issued a very discouraging order in which the subject of the four classes and thirty six caste of Nepal were forbidden to go to India for recruitment. All the Nepali subjects willing to join the Indian Army needed Nepal Durbar's prior approval. In this order it was clearly stated that any Nepali who disobeyed would have his house and land confiscated. It was also stated that a soldier who violated the order would not be entitled to punish his wife's lover if she had any. A soldier working in the Indian Army was also liable to capital punishment if he killed the lover of his wife.[6] Hence, in no way can Mr. W.

B. Horthey's assessment of the Nepali situation be acceptable. The main intention of Jang Bahadur's policy was to maintain a double standard, which can clearly be seen in his letter dated 1858 to the District Officer, Krishna Dhoj:

> Without letting the Saheb (British Officer) know, issue an order to the Gurkhas of our country not to visit Almoda to join the (British) Army. Also write to the Saheb stating that it is not correct to force any one for recruitment but if someone wishes to enlist willingly, he will not be stopped.[7]

Another issue which discouraged the British recruitment was Jang Bahadur's refusal to co-operate the British in tracing the heirs of deceased Gurkha soldiers. In this context Jang Bahadur's despatch to Resident George Ramsay is worth quoting:

> I often receive Yaddashts (reminders) from you requesting me to trace the heirs of deceased Goorkhalese, men who had enlisted in the British Army. I therefore beg that, in order to obviate such useless annoyance and trouble, you will be so good as to cause such requisitions to be discontinued by representing these cir cumstances to His Excellency the Viceroy and Governor General.[8]

Thus, despite Jang Bahadur's diplomatic discouragements, during his period of Prime Ministership two additional Gurkha regiments (4th and 5th) were raised and the recruits required for maintaining all the five Gurkha Regiments were recruited indirectly without the prior knowledge and permission of the government of Nepal.

The sudden death of Jang Bahadur on 25 February 1877, the possibility of Anglo-Afgan War (1878) and British attempt of strengthening Armed forces to protect their interests in the neighbouring Indian states were a few of those causes that shaped the inner mechanism of the Anglo-Nepalese relations in later half of the nineteenth century. The emergence of a weak and godfearing Prime Minister Ranoudip Singh further caused the major shifts in the history of Gurkha recruitment. However, Jang

Bahadur's policy of isolation, friendly co-operation and firm attitude on certain issues towards the British found its relevance in this phase in the vital role played by Dhir Shumshere in administrating the Nepal Darbar.

Ranoudip Singh immediately after assuming his office declared his intension of adopting the policies laid down by his predecessor. In the words of Resident Henvey:

> He had been entirely in the confidence of late Sir Jang Bahadur, who had exhorted and instructed him to persue the same course of steady and undeviating friendship towards the British Government.[9]

The most significant event that initiated a round of transactions of Gurkha recruitment in this phase of history was the outbreak of second Anglo-Afgan War. As soon as Renoudip Singh learned through newspapers about the possibility of this war, he offered military help to the British Government. It proved to be an apt excuse to exert required pressure on Nepal Darbar to meet the immediate need for at least one thousand Gurkha recruits.[10] In this context, Impey, the then Resident to Nepal, tried to persuade Dhir Shumshere that what the British government wanted was not the regular troops which Ranoudip Singh had offered. In Impey's view what was more important was the withdrawal of all existing restrictions on the entry of the Gurkhas into the British services. The British government wanted to regularise the whole recruiting procedure. Hence, the desire of Impey was to formulate a policy through which the Nepalese government itself could recruit and supply the British their required force.

But the principal thrust of Dhir Shumshere (and thus of Ŗanoudip Singh) was to be in confidence of late Sir Jang Bahadur who had instructed to pursue the same course of steady and undeviating friendship towards the British government. Hence, Impey's proposal could not make considerable influence on the staunch followers of late

The Gurkha soldiers from 2/6th Gurkhas advance on the Italian Front.

Range firing party waiting to hear their scores

A Gurkha soldier on the Italian front during World War II.

The Jubiliant riflemen of the 7th Duke of Edinburgh's Own Rifles

Men of the 7th Gurkhas in the Folkland War

Two Gurkha riflemen on the Italian front in January 1944.

Jung Bahadur. In regard to Impey's proposal Dhir Shumshere argued that the Gurkhas did not want to serve anywhere outside the country because this meant deserting their families and polluting their religious belief. Dhir also lamented on the crafty functioning of British recruiting agents in tempting Gurkhas already serving in the Nepalese army.

Despite these frustrating moves of Nepal Durbar in restricting the recruitments, Resident Impey managed to get from Ranoudip Singh only 559 men after 6 months of persuasion. Three hundred and thirty nine soldiers out of these were rejected because they were declared "the lame, the halt, the maimed and the blind." Thus, in order to procure this small number of recruits, the British had to spend nearly Rs.13,600 including the expenses of rejected candidates to return to their homes.[11]

In addition to this, the commanding officers of Gurkha Regiments blamed the recruiting system for its inefficiency and unpredictability. They were also ambivalent towards the question of including the inferior tribes like Sudwars and Rais at the expense of letting these Regiments far below their full strength. The whole predicament is expressed by Colonal Sail Hill, a veteran officer of the first Gurkhas, in the following extract:

> If the Nepal Darbar supplies us with recruits similar to those lately received we shall either have to reject them at an expense to the state or to flood our ranks with a class of men that will deteriorate Gorkha Regiments.[12]

In order to regularise the recruiting process systematically, Resident Gridlestone made a number of proposals to the British authorities. One of the proposals was to offer 'head money' to Nepal Darbar for every fit recruit. He also recommended that the less martial tribes of Nepal and the natives from Kumaon, Garhwal and Punjab hillstate too should be given a chance of serving in the Gurkha Regiments. Another important suggestion that the Resident offered to the British Indian government was that the recruited soldiers should be allowed to carry their wives and children along with them. He also suggested that the pensioners from the Gurkha Regiments should be given healthy encouragements to settle in the British territories. The whole point was to procure recruits from the families growing up in a Gurkha cantonement for the Indian Army.

The first proposal was rejected on financial grounds. The British government found it impossible to offer 'head money' for each fit recruit. The second proposal too was rejected for the British Military authorities did not want to effect the efficiency of the Regiments by mixing less martial tribes with the pure Gurkhas. Lastly, the idea of allowing the recruits to keep their families with them too was rejected for the fear that Nepal Government would never accept it.

Hence, *Sub rosa* operations were considered most appropriate for the time being with the hope that a good opportunity for systematic recruitment would be available soon.[13]

Contrary to the British expectations the opportunities for getting new recruits were strangled by the Nepalese Government to curb the British efforts, strict measures were implemented. Throughout the country a census was taken of the military tribes; the village Head was ordered to prevent anyone leaving Nepal without the Royal permission; house to house inquiry was made and names of all adult males were noted carefully; the families of those who had sneaked into the British Army were tortured and the retired Gurkha soldiers found it difficult to draw their pensions.The Nepalese Government ordered the execution of those recruiting agents who were at work on the borders.[14] Regarding this situation Resident Gridlestone wrote:

> Whereas formerly men caught in Nepal recruiting for us (British) were to be bound and sent to British territory, they are now to be cut in two. Men are sent about in disguise, badly dressed and apparently in great want, and if asked by a recruiting agent to enlist, they immediately turn round and seize him. He is kept in custody then, and gets anything but gentle treatment.[15]

The soldiers who had come on leave were induced by a combination of persuasion and slight pressure not to return to their jobs. Those who defied the orders were punished. To expose the inner mechanism of the Nepal Darbar's hostile policies in suppressing the recruitment, the case of one Johar Sing who had gone to join the British Indian Army without Nepal Darbar's permission can be cited. On his return to Nepal during leave, Johar Singh was arrested and sentenced to 23 months imprisonment. His property too was confiscated and he was forced to sign an agreement under pressure in which Johar singh accepted to be liable to punishment if he went to join the British Indian Army again.[16]

What Gridlestone wanted the military authorities to give up were the calendestine operations. Though the authorities agreed that the recruiting procedure was unsystematic and unsatisfactory, they opposed such an attitude for the fear of war. They were also not ready to raise this issue with Nepal Darbar because it only meant inflating the importance of Gurkhas without any material gain. But, disappointed,Gridlestone was absolutely sure that no proper recruitment could be had unless the Nepal Darbar itself helped in the major recruiting operations. In addition to this, Resident Gridlestone displayed his dissatisfaction with the priority that British Government gave to Magars and Gurungs as recruits. He was of the opinion that the other races of Nepal too were capable of displaying an exquisite show of valour.

By 1879, there were five Gurkha Regiments with 16 Gorkha officers and 85 Sepoys in each Regiment. The total number of the Gurkhas in the British Indian Army was 4,685 men.[17] The first, second, third, fourth and fifth Gurkha Regiments were encamped at Dharam Salah, Bakoh, Dehradun, Almora and Abbotabad.[18] Besides this, a large number of Gurkhas served in the 42nd, 43rd, 44th infantry Regiments.[19]

An important instance that encouraged the move of 'Arms for Gurkha' was Nepal's fear of a war with Tibet. In 1884 the Nepali Government gave a rare opportunity to the British when it asked for 4000 Breach loading weapans to fight the Tibetians.[20] Though the foreign department and the Governor General were fascinated by the proposal the Council was divided on the issue. One of the members, A. Colvin, argued the possibility of exciting suspicions and shattering the friendly relations with Nepal if the British Government pressed her for recruits. When the Secretary of State refused to make any concrete decision on the issue, the Governor General's Council in the end was left at "liberty to open negotiation and to offer the Nepalese Government 4000 Sinders with ammunitions". The Secretary of the state reflected his predicament in the following words:

> I am very sensible of increasing the Gorkha element in the native army, and I consider that any arrangement which would remove the obstacles at present interposed to the free enlistment of recruits of this race, would be of such value as to justify concession to the Nepalese Durbar in the matter of arms of precision .... .[21]

Though foreign secretary C. Grant had urged the Viceroy to supply arms to Nepal immediately, the whole move could not be materialised because Nepal's dispute with Tibet had already been settled. The Nepal Government's request for arms to confront Tibet synchronised with the British Government's urgency for recruits to protect themselves against the Russian threat. To meet this unpredictable situation, the British Government decided that the efficiency and bulk of the army should be increased, and maximum priority was given to the Gurkhas. It had already been decided that, while all other Regiments would have 832 men, the Gurkha corps would have 912 in each Regiment.

The Death of Dhir Shumshere in October 1884 marked the beginning of Ranoudip Singh's liberal attitude towards the Gurkha recruitment issue. At this moment, the Indian Government too decided to increase the number of Gurkha Battalions from 5 to 10, adding a second battalion to each Regiment.[22] It was here that Ranoudip Singh offered the help of ten to fifteen thousand Nepalese troops to the British to be used in Sudan and Afganistan:

> I deem it necessary to maintain an army of 15,000 more in Nepal, and drill them to make a splendid rescue, and that the British Government would pay for it at the rate of Rs. seven per each private, and to the officers according to their ranks.

The Prime Minister also sent a delegation of top officials to Rawalpindi to pay respect to the Viceroy assuring military help promised by him earlier. Though the Viceroy did not want to waste money on recruiting troops who would be of no use to the British in future, he immediately requested the Prime Minister to facilitate the supply to the Gurkha Regiments in the British services. Resident Gridlestone clearly explained that what his government needed was the Gurkha recruits and not the regular Nepali troops. He further argued that it would take six months to train the Nepali troops on British model and thus would not be able to use them immediately.[24] When Ranoudip expressed his difficulty in collecting 15000 recruits, the Resident argued that he saw no difference between collecting 15000 men for reserve or for recruitment. This set of negotiations between Gridlestone and the top officials of Nepal led to the following demands formulated by the Resident under the instruction for the Indian Government:

(a) Permission for British Recruiting Agents to enlist men for the British army at all times in Nepal, irrespective of fixed numbers and caste.

(b) Permission for retired and pensioned soldiers to settle in their own country upon the termination of their active service.

(c) Untrained permission for soldiers to visit their homes in Nepal during the period of their service.[25]

Furthermore, Gridlestone asked General Kedar Narsingh to offer 5660 recruits immediately for the additional battalions, and 1300 every year to fill the vacancy. In return Gridlestone assured to give 4000 Sinders with ammunitions free of cost.

Dissatisfied with these minor concessions, Ranoudip Singh lamented on his failure to get the British title of G.C.B. which had been awarded to Jang Bahadur. Besides, General Kedar NarSingh strongly demanded "a strip of land in the plains to the south of boundry which now runs at the foot of Danduwa hill between Oudh and Nepal."[26] Renoudip also objected to the admission of recruiting parties to Nepal. He did not want the establishment of any Army Depots at the Capital because that might frustrate his efforts and deprive him of any credit obtained in the matter.[27]

Despite these grudges Ranoudip Singh agreed to reach an agreement according to which Nepal was prepared:

1. To circulate the notice to the recruits throughout the country, proclaiming that whoever is willing to take military service under the British Government is at full liberty to do so on condition of previously making the local Nepalese district officers acquainted with his intention.

2. To supply the copies of such proclaimations, if desired to the British recruiting Agents, who may

be on the lookout for recruits near the frontier on the British side, inorder to facilitate their proceedings.

3. To exert itself to collect recruits, but owing to previous want of success in similar efforts to meet Lord Lytton's recruitments, and by reason of the fact that the Nepalese standing army is said to be at present some 700 to 800 men below strength, the minister wishes it to be understood that he is not sanguine of great results.

4. To allow pensioners from British Gurkha and Assam regiments to collect recruits under the supervision of Prime Minister of Nepal.

5. To permit the surgeon of Residency to examine all candidates, and to accept his opinion regarding physical fitness of otherwise as conclusive.

6. To agree to the training of recruits as a temporary measure, under the supervision of Resident by the Regident's escort on the Residency parade ground, or the Prime Minister of Nepal will arrange for such training in accordance with the system now observed in respect of British Native troops on his own parade ground by men of the Nepalese Army, who have previously served under the British flag.[28]

Having succeeded in persuading Nepal Darbar, Gridlestone recommended inducements to be offered to it to make the above quoted agreement a successful reality. To materialise this, several inducement such as the grant of breach-loading rifles, permission to import lead and sulpher for the Nepalese troops, confering upon the Prime Minister of a G.C.S.I. or G.C.B., a salute of 19 guns and Cession of a strip of Terai Land on the frontier were recommended by Gridlestone. Accepting the first three recommen dations with some provisions the British

Government dismissed the question of the cession of land and the Resident was in structed to remain silent about this issue.[29]

The positive dialogue of understanding between the British and the Nepal Darbar was disrupted with the transfer of Gridlestone to Mysore for some months. The tough attitude of the officiating Resident Colonel Berkley suspended the series of successful transaction between the two parties. Though the Nepalese Government, satisfied with the assurence given by Gridlestone, tried sincerely to collect recruits for the British, Colonel Berkley found some fault with the working of the Nepalese Government. While collecting recruits the Nepalese Government had stated that "no body is required to do so" (enlist in the British service); and that "those who on now being asked do not agree to enlist, and after words go to by stealth, will be considered guilty of deceit and punished."[30]

Colonel Berkley complained that such language would discourage Nepalese from joining the British Services and charged the Prime Minister with violating the aggrement which obliged the Nepal Government to remove all restrictions on recruitment question. The officiating Resident himself drafted the proposed announcement, in which it was stated that "the Nepalese Government will be pleased with those who go to enlist".[31] In the end only 800 recruits were collected within a few months. To the resident's demand for able and sufficient recruits, Ranoudip Singh admitted his failure in getting more but assured to increase the recruits in getting more but assured to increase the recruits in getting more but assured to increase the recruits in large numbers if the British arranged the medical test somewhere near the border in the East and West. Though the suggestion was accepted, it could not take a practical shape because by this time Ranoudip Singh had already been assassinated and the sword of power had fallen in the hands of the Second Generation of Ranas.

References

1. *Historical Records of the 5th Gurkha Regiment,* Lahor, 1886, p.170.

2. Leo. E. Rose, *Op, Cit.*, p. 133.

3. Napier Papers, Vol. 5/3, (quoted in Kanchanmoy Mojumdar, *Politi cal Relations between India and Nepal,* pp.42-43).

4. Christopher Chant, *Op. Cit.,* pp.43-44.

5. W.B. Northey, *Land of Gurkhas,* Cambridge, 1937, p.77.

6. Leo. E. Rose, *Nepal; Strategy for Survival, Delhi* Oxford University Press, 1973, p. 133.

7. Abstract translation of a letter from Jang Bahadur to district officer Krishna Dhoj. dated 1858 (quoted in Chita Ranjan Nepali "Nepal Ra British Gorkha Rifles", *Ruprekha,* Vol. 40,p.13).

8. Abstract translation of a Yaddastha from Maharajah Jang Bahadur Rana to the address of Colonel George Ramsay, Resident at Nepal, dated 11th of Jeyt Sambat 1923 (June 9, 1966), *Foreign Department Political,* July 1866, No.65, (N.A.I.).

9. *Foreign Secret,* December, 1877 No.104, (N.A.I.).

10. *Foreign Political A.* February 1879, No.245 (N.A.I.).

11. *Foreign Political A*. March 1880, No. 98-99, (quoted in Tri-Ratna Manandhar, Nepal; the years of trouble, p.185).

12. K. Mojumdar, *Political Relations between India and Nepal (1877-1923),* Delhi, 1973, p.45.

13. *Foreign Political A,* March 1880, No.95-110, (N.A.I.).

14. *Ibid.*, July 1880, No.70, (quoted in Tri-Ratna Manandhar, *Op. Cit.,* pp.187-88).

15. *Ibid.*

16. *Foreign Political B.* April 1882, No.70 (quoted in Tri-Ratna Ma nandhar, *Op.Cit.*, pp. 187-88).

17. *Foreign Department Proceedings,* March 1880, 95-110, quoted in sushila Tyagi *Op. Cit.,* p. 204.

18. *Foreign Department Proceedings,* July 1880, 141-58, quoted in Sushila Tyagi *Op. Cit.*, p.204.

19. *Ibid,* March 1880.
20. *Foreign Secret E.*, June 1884, No.438, (N.A.I.).
21. *Foreign Secret E.*, November, 1884, No.234. (N.A.I.).
22. *Ibid,* April 1885 No.84 (N.A.I).
23. *Ibid,* No.94.
24. Resident to Prime Minister, April 9, 1885, *Foreign Ministry Nepal,* Poka 97.
25. *Foreign Secret E.* April 1885, No.78 (N.A.I.).
26. *Foreign Secret E.* July 1885 no.47 (N.A.I.).
27. *Ibid.,* no.45.
28. *Ibid.,* no.37.
29. *Ibid.,* no.51.
30. *Foreign Department's Sanad,* 1942 B.S. (June 1885) no. 38, RNAH.
31. *Prime Minister's Order,* August, 1885, no.38 RNAH.

Pressure

CHAPTER FIVE

The emergence of Shumshere family as the de facto rulers of Nepal by a blood-stained coup on 22 November 1885 provided the British a golden opportunity to solve the problem of Gurkha recruitment. The new Nepalese Prime Minister Bir Shumshere anxiously wanted to secure British recognition of his new regime. He was also afraid that his cousions who had taken shelter in India, may try to use British help to regain their lost authority in Nepal. Such a shaky position of Bir Shumshere forced him to abandon the policy of nationalism and British isolation set by Jang Bahadur and his successors. In order to keep his enemies at the bay, he had to maintain a warm and promising relations with the British. The British administration on the other hand was not unanimous on the question of giving recognition to the new Government in Nepal. Commander-in-Chief Roberts, Secretary H.M. Durand and Resident Gridlestone wanted to fully exploit the initial instabilities of the new regime.[1] The British Government, which was threatened by the deteriorating relations with Russia, wanted the expansion of their Army. Roberts, the then Commander-in-Chief of India, proposed to raise five additional Gurkha Battalions as soon as possible. He also suggested that the only way to get recruits within a reasonable span of time was to open recruiting depots at Kathmandu and to put adequate pressure on Nepal Darbar to allow the British recruiting agents to operate in the hills of Nepal.[2] He urged the foreign department to deal with Bir Shumshere plainly and firmly. He should be threatened, Roberts was of the opinion, of his removal if he did not supply the Gurkha recruits promptly, and that, the Commander-in-Chief added, would be done with British help to Bir Shumshere's rivals living in exile. He was also in favour of giving some money to Nepal in lieu of the Gurkha recruits.[3] But Bir Shumshere who had already anticipated this situation, started supplying the recruits in adequate numbers. As a result of which within a month of his rise to power, Bir Shumshere supplied 700 recruits.[4] The suspicion and anger of the British authorities towards the new regime was pacified to some extent by this initial enthusiasm of Bir Sumshere in supplying the recruits. Colonel J.C. Berkeley, the acting Resident in Kathmandu, played an important role in endowing recognition on the new Rana regime in Nepal. He wrote:

> Jang Bahadur was steeped in blood and the present Minister and his family are as bad as they can be, but they had already rendered us service, and it is conceivable that they might be able to do as much for us as Jang Bahadur did.[5]

He strongly recommended for the recognition of Bir's regime in the following words:

> Unless we mean to change our whole policy towards Nepal, and to abandon strict neutrality for active interference, it seems to me that it does not matter to us which set of cut-throats has the upper hand.[6]

Finally, in the beginning of 1886, the British Government in India granted recognition to the new Rana regime in Nepal. Here, initial co-operation in recruitment and anxiety for British recognition does not mean that Bir Shumshere was pro-British. Infact there was no foundamental change in Nepal's policy towards the British. Moreover, Shumshere family had the reputation of being hostile to the British. Dhir Shumshere, father of Bir Shumshere, was always taken as anti-British. He had strongly opposed Jang Bahadur's support of British duing the Indian Muti ny. Hence, Bir Shumshere in heart of his heart was never willing to divert from Nepal's traditional policy of isolation. But to the British government he gave full assurance to help in the matter of recruitment.

In order to facilitate the British desire of strengthening the Gurkha Regiments, Bir Shumshere not only granted his approval to raise five more Gurkha Battalions, but also tried his best to supply sufficient number of recruits. Prior to 1886, there was no centralised system of Gurkha recruitment. In 1886 in order to systematise and to simplify the recruiting process a sanction was accorded for the establishment of Gurkha recruiting depot at Gorakhpur. It was first depot of its kind in India.[7] But assur ances, given by Bir Shumshere to facilitate recruiting process, did little in removing the British suspicions. What British authorities wanted was some permanent solution to this problem. Accordingly a proposal was made to Nepalese Prime Minister Bir Shumshere in 1886 by officiating Resident Berkley in which it was thought that if the Gurkhas already serving in the Indian Army were allowed to bring their families to India, the supply of the required recruits in future can be fulfilled to some extent by enlisting their children. But this proposal was rejected by Bir Shumshere on the following grounds:

> 'Istly. This proposal (if carried out) will necessiate the departure from Nipal of a considerable number of families at the present time and of more than two or three hundred families annually in future and these will consist of Magars and Gurungs who are scanty in Nepal. For you (British officers) annually enlist more than three or four hundred recruits, consisting more of men of the Gurung and Magar clans and less of men of other tribes, in view to the filling up of casualties. It is certain that these will also wish to take their families with themselves.
>
> '2ndly. The Nipalese subjects who were enlisted in British regiments, and who were trained in the British service, used on obtaining pension to come back to Nipal for the purpose

of joining their families and the serving in the Nipalese army for a while they used to impart instruction to others. If the families of these men go to British India, and make it their home and dwell there, they will have then no necessity at all to return to Nipal.

'3rdly. When there remains no necessity for those men to return hither the benefits which it is hoped would accrue to other subjects of this Government through the earning of money in British territory by such men and the spending of it in Nipal after they have obtained pension will not be realized.

'4thly. The Darbar has had to overlook and ignore the quarrels which took place between the people and such sepoys as were deputed on recruiting duty, and which resulted from the discon tent of the people under extreme pressure that had to be employed in view of complying with the wishes of the British Government for the collecting and bringing forward as many recruits as possible. If, therefore, efforts were to be made at present in this matter, the people of this country being, as a rule, devoid of intelligence would consider that the Darbar, unmindful of its own interests, was using its utmost influence in endeavours to expel also the families of its subjects from this country. Consequently the proposal is not calculated to result in any good to Nipal.

'5thly. The benefits which colonel Berkeley said that Nipal will reap from the training and the pension which the Nipalese sepoy would obtain will thus be illusory.[8]

However, with his deep rooted conviction of not to displease the British administration, Bir Shumshere not only prompted but also used force as well to obtain required number of recruits. The first step that he took in getting recruits was to offer money for the consent of the natives. When this failed, a regulation was proclaimed in which each Nepalese village was forced to supply a fixed number of recruits. In addition to this, Darbar was made to procure the service of additional number of Government officers and sepoys.[9]

This rigorous regulation not only failed in getting the required supply of recruits but also made the recruiting extremely unpopular. In this process the credibility of Nepal Darbar administration too was in danger. The villagers started fighting with the Darbar's recruiting parties. In the end, to Bir Shumshere's disappointment, out of seven or eight thousand men who appeared before the Army Doctor only 2200 were found physically fit for recruitment. In the same year (1886), with these recruits, three new Gurkha Regiments namely, 42nd Regiment Gurkha Light Infantry, 43rd Regiment Gorkha Light Infantry and 44th Regiment Goorkha Light Infantry, were added to the existing four Gurkha Regiments. However, Bir Shumshere, disappointed with the situation tried to convince the British Indian authority in the following words:

> My friends, since I have been looking out for means to please the British government I should not have hesitated to a thing, had it not been beyond my powers.[10]

Repeating his assurance of supplying the adequate number of recruits, he stated:

> ...I write to assure that I will again issue encouraging notifications and orders to the Nepalese officers on the borders to countenance, without fail, such men as wish to accept service under the British Government, and to make it generally known that in the eyes of the Durbar persons who accept the British service will be regarded as though they had accepted service under the Durbar.[11]

This encouraging attitude of Nepal Darbar, however, stiffened with the return of Gridlestone from his officiating appointment at Mysore. On July 13, 1886, he took charge from the acting Resident at Kathmandu. With his arrival he flared the suspicion of Shumshere family, which held Gridlestone as a foremost sympa thizer of the exiled Jang family. Hence, the crack of suspicion appeared between the two parties. Resident Gridlestone reported his feelings in the following words:

> My conviction is that the present administration has not our interest at heart, and that even if it had its modus operandi would be more likely to do us harm than good in the long run.[12]

However, the efforts of Bir Shumshere had a very good result in the recruiting season of 1886-87. Regarding the recruitment situation of the year 1886-87, Resident Girdlestone reported:

> I believe, a far higher return, numerical and proportional, for filling vacancies than that of any previous year; and by dint of the efforts used the percentage of Magars and Gurungs for the line battalions has been more than maintained.[13]

The important feature of this year's recruitment was that almost all the recruits came of their own freewill and Nepalese Govern ment did not have to use any force. But the hostile relation of Gridlestone with Bir Shumshere was taken as a serious matter of concern by British administration in India. Aware of this situation, Lord Dufferin, the then Governor General of India, removed Gridlestone in early 1888 to prevent the further crackdowns. Major E.L. Durand was appointed the new Resident to Nepal.[14] The tenure of office of Major Durand as Resident was also not a very happy one. From the very beginning, he had a very bad opinion of Bir Shumshere's rule.

Hence, to have direct talks with the Governor General, Bir Shum shere paid visit to Calcutta in February 1888 and reassured Lord Dufferin of the regular supply of recruits to the Indian Army.[15] The Viceroy inturn assured the Prime Minister that his government will not meddle with internal affairs of Nepal. He also promised to impose stricter survilliance on the young Ranas living in exile in India. Hence Bir Shumshere's insecure position always prompted the Governor General to maintain warm reciprocity.

In 1888 when Nepal Darbar claimed for the expense incurred on the accounts of recruits enlisted in the Gurkha Battalions in India, the British Government proposed a

A Bren gunner of the 7th Gurkha Rifles in the Burma jungle in 1942.

The Gurkha soldiers in France.

Lance-Corporal Ram Bahadur Limbu, 10th Princess Mary's Own Gurkha Rifles, with his son.

The men of the 7th Gurkhas travelling on the liner Queen Elizabeth 2

bonus of Rupees 20/- to Nepal Durbar for every recruit approved through British agency.[16] Lateron, it expressed its desire to give a Sinder rifle for every recruit obtained on the year 1888 upto the limit of 5000.

Encouraged by the recruiting activities, Eden Vansittart, the recruiting officer at Gorakhapur depot, proposed to the Resident that there should be a recruiting depot at Kathmandu itself. He also pointed out that with the establishment of a recruiting depot at Kathmandu, the recruiting could go throughout the year. The proposal, thoroughly discussed by the Foreign Ministry, was put before Bir Shumshere. Eden Vansittart was also proposed to be appointed as military assistant to the Resident during summer, and not a recruiting officer. But if some recruits presented themselves for enlistment at the Residency during the summer, the military assistant was entitled to enlist them. Actually what the British government had in mind was to carry out the process of recruitment throughout the year with the help of a military officer who in disguise would keep playing the role of recruiting officer as well. Here the main intention of the British government was to pave the way for a permanent recruiting depot at kathmandu. But Bir Shumshere knew it very well. Hence, he rejected the proposal in the following words:

> In regard to enlisting recruits who may present themselves for enlistment in the Residency during the summer, I am indeed very sorry to say that I am unable to agree to this proposal.[17]

Soon after the rejection of proposal by Bir Shumshere, Resident Major Durand, the chief supporter of the proposal, was also replaced by Colonal H. Wylie as Resident in Nepal (1891).[18]

By now, Lord Dufferin's policy of mutual understanding had already won the confidence of Bir Shumshere, which ultimately helped Lansdowne and Elgin to bring him closer to the British Government. The new Resident Colonel Wylie was also instructed by the Governor General to follow the policy of conciliation and compromise. This marks the beginning of a new phase of mutual co-operation and accomodation in the Anglo-Nepalese relations.

References

1. Durand to Col. I.C. Berkeley, *Officiating Resident,* 30 November, 1885.
2. K. Mojumdar, *Political Relations between India and Nepal,* p.54.
3. *Ibid.*
4. *Bir to Dilli Shamsher Jang Thapa,* 1942 B.S. (December 1885) RNAH. no.35.
5. Berkeley to Cuningham, dated Residency Baroda, January 4, 1887, (Confidential) Demi-Official, *Foreign Secret-E,* February 1887, no.504, (N.A.I.).(quoted in Asad Husain *op.cit.*)
6. *Foreign Secret E*, February 1887, no.405, (N.A.I.).(*Ibid*)
7. C.T. Morries, *Gurkha-Hand Book for the India Armies,* Manager of Publication, Delhi, 1936, p.130.
8. *Foreign Department Secret Proceedings-E*, December 1886, No.11-12, (N.A.I.) (quoted in Asad Husain), *Op. Cit.*, p.245.
9. Sushila Tyagi, *Op. Cit.,* pp. 134-135.
10. *Abstract translation of a Yaddasht from the Prime Minister and commander-in-Chief of Nepal, to the Resident in Nepal.* Dated Poos 5th Sumvat 1943 (December 16, 1886), Reed December 20, 1886, *Foreign Department Secret Proceedings,* February 1887, no. 162 (N.A.I.) (quoted in Asad Husain Op. cit., p.246).
11. *Foreign Department Proceedings-E* February 1887, No. 62 (quoted in Asad Husain Ibid.).
12. *Foreign Department Secret Proceedings-E,* February 1887, no.161, (N.A.I.) (quoted in Asad Husain *Ibid*).
13. *Ibid,* September 1887, no. 113, (N.A.I.).

14. K. Mazumdar, *Political Relation between India and Nepal,* p.56.

15. *Ibid.*

16. *Ibid.*

17. Proposal to appoint an officer as Military Assistant to the Resident in Nepal in Connection with Gurkhas Recruiting Captain E. Vansittart selected for the post, *Foreign Department Secret- E,* February 1892, Nos. 315-20 (N.A.I.).(quoted in Asad Husain *op.cit.*)

18. Asad Husain, *Op. Cit.,* p.135.

Introspection

CHAPTER SIX

The last decade of the 19h century marked the beginning of a significant change in the British attitude towards Nepal. They had already realised the failure of their pressure politics and had decided to adopt a new policy of winning Nepalese confidence by offering liberal concessions. In fact, what the British Government wanted was to remove the grave mutual distrust existing between the two Governments. The main British objective in Nepal during this period also remained the fulfillment of the requirement of Gurkha recruits. Though the co-operative attitude of Bir Shumshere had already resulted into a satisfactory recruiting arrangements, Commander-in-Chief Roberts, who had earlier advocated a strong policy towards Nepal, was not satisfied with the overall supply of the recruits. Inorder to win the Nepalese goodwill, Roberts put forward a number of proposals. For instance, he offered to send British officers to train the Nepalese troops at Kathmandu, to attach a Nepalese Battalion, to the Indian Regiments and to give the Nepalese officers honorary commission in the British Gurkha Regiments. Roberts was of the opinion that these measures would be popular with the Gurkha troops in India which ultimately would stimulate recruiting in Nepal.[1]

The appointment of colonel Wylie as Resident to Nepal worked as a catalyst in furthering the new British policy of conciliation and compromise. From the very beginning he started his work in the line of developing mutual understanding. In a letter to the Secretary to the Government of India, Colonel Wylie clearly wrote:

> The position of affair when I first went to Kathmandu in 1891 may be described as one of the grave-mutual distrust between our government and that of Nepal, and knowing how perfectly sincere we were in our desire to be on friendly terms with that state and also that we have no ulterior designs upon it, I believed it to be my duty to endeavour to bring about a better understanding between ourselves and the Durbar.[2]

In addition to this account of the existing state of Indo-Nepalese affairs, Resident Wylie condemned the scheme of appointing a recruiting officer as military assistant to the Resident in Nepal:

> If Captain Vansittart comes here with any idea of recruiting, he will come in the teeth of the very strongest protest from the Nepalese Prime Minister, and will probably arouse great ill-feeling throughout the Durbar.[3]

Not only this, Resident Wylie also expressed his satisfaction on the state of supply of recruits by Bir Shumshere and argued with the Government of India on the inadvisability of getting a friendly Prime Minister into trouble:

> Considering all he has done for us in the way of recruiting, we can now say (if necessary) that, after considering these objections and out of personal regard to himself, we will not now press the appointment of Captain Vansittart, but we expect the Matharaja to continue to help us with recruiting, as if, under the present system, the numbers of recruits fall off, we will have to consider whether it will not be necessary to take other steps to ensure a full supply. If a spur is needed this will probably keep him up to the collar.[4]

Resident Wylie's new diplomacy paid off. After he took over the Residentship in Nepal, the Indian Army got more Gurkha recruits than ever before. The recruiting operations were systematised. Besides, the establishment of a central recruiting depot of Gorakhpur other recruiting depots were also opened at Darjeeling, Pilibhit and Bahraich. The enlistment of Rais and Limbus from eastern Nepal also started. By 1892 there were already 10 Gurkha Regiments serving in India. Altogether 7,662 Gurkha recruits were supplied in 1886-92, mostly Magars and Gurungs.[5] Resident Wylie highly appreciated the co-operation of Bir Shumshere in the supply of recruits:

> ... for this continued improvement in recruitment, we have to thank Maharaja Bir Shamsher, as it is only since his accession to power that we have succeeded in filling our ranks with the best classes of Gurkhas.[6]

But Bir Shumshere always opposed the idea of keeping Indian Army reservists in Nepal.

Meanwhile another important event which helped in removing the mutual distrust was the visit of Commander-in-Chief Roberts to Kathmandu in March 1892. This was for the first time that a high ranking British military officer paid a visit to Kathmandu. Roberts was impressed by the humble manners and administrative efficiency of Bir Shumshere. Lord Roberts, summing up his impressions of Nepal, Wrote:

> Notwithstanding the occasional differences which have occurred between our Government and the Nepal Durbar, I believe that, ever since 1817, (1815-16) when the Nepal war was brought to a successful conclusion by Sir David Ochterlony, the Gurkhas have had a great respect and liking for us; but they are in perpetual dread of our taking their country, and they think the only way to prevent this is not to allow anyone to enter it except by invitation, and to insist upon the few thus favoured travelling by the difficult route that we traversed Nepal can never be required by us for defensive purposes, and as we get our best class of Native soldiers thence, everything should, I think, be done to show our confidence in the Nepalese alliance, and convince them that we have no ulterior designs on the independence of their kingdom.[7]

The visit was followed by a return visit which Bir Shumshere made in February 1893. Colonel Wylie also proposed that the title of K.C.S.I be conferred on Bir Shumshere for his outstanding support to the British Government. Governor General Lansdowne who was closely watching all these developments secured a K.C.S.I. (Knight Commander of the Star of India) for Bir in May 1892 as the mark of appreciation of his policy towards the British.[8] In order to propagate the policy of mutual concessions, the British administration after a series of transactions agreed to give 8000 Martiny-Henry Rifles and Six 7 pounder field guns desired by Bir Shumshere.[9]

The major objectives of British government by this time were to increase facilities for getting Gurkha recruits and the removal of the restrictions placed on the movement of British Resident in Nepal. Promising help to Nepalese Government in procuring arms and ammunitions from India and England the British Government not only worked to liberate the trade and to make Nepal accessible for Europeans but also was able to get the desired number of recruits of selected tribes from Nepal with the due support of Nepal Darbar. Bir's benevolent efforts got further recognition, when he was made a G.C.S.I. (Grand Cross of Star of India) in 1897. Though during the Prime Ministership of Bir Shumshere no definite agreement was concluded with regard to Gurkha recruitment, the recruiting parties were made free to work in the country. Bir Shumshere even circulated a notice throughout the Kingdom for procuring recruits needed for Indian Army. The following words of Bir Shumshere aptly capture the essence of the reality existent in the successful functioning of Wylie's new diplomacy:

> ...the late Maharajas, Sir Jung Bahadur and Sir Ranoudip Singh Rana had not the courage to supply recruits to the British Government, yet with the view of strengthening the basis of friendship with the British Government, I as far as

possible, having explained to and satisfied the Bharadars and arranged that the raitis (peasants) would not be displeased, have carried on the work with facility.[10]

The turn of the century not only found the Anglo-Nepalese relations on a more friendly footings, the policy of mutual understanding and mutual concessions also got a solid foundation for its further flourishment. Wylie was replaced in 1899 by Lt. Colonel W. Loch as Resident to Nepal. The British Government's desire to win the Nepal Darbar's confidence is evident from the following extract from a report by new Resident W. Loch in 1900:

> ...I believe the Darbar is inclined to relax its policy of mistrust, certainly the Resident is not dogged about by spies to the extent complained of formerly, and a certain amount of latitude is extended to me in allowing me to visit parts of the country off the beaten track of visitors for the purpose of fishing. I am inclined to follow my predecessor's plan which was to work patiently to win the Darbar's confidence, rely on it for information and refrain from trying to obtain information through channels of my own.[11]

The sudden death of Bir Shumshere on March 5, 1901 resulted into a brief political turmoil in Nepal. He was succeeded by his brother Dev Shumshere and the three months duration of Dev Shumshere's Prime Ministership was usurped by Chandra Shumshere in a bloodless coup on 25 June 1901. The clash of Dev Shumshere's progressive ideas with the towering ambition of Chandra Shumshere shaped the major trends of early twenteeth century Nepalese administration. In order to strengthen his position at home Chandra Shumshere openly opted for an extremely positive attitude towards the British. In a letter to the Viceroy he wrote:

> I shall take this opportunity of assuring your Excellency's Government that I shall always deem it a sacred duty and valued privilege, not only to cultivate and continue unimpaired the friendly relations subsisting between the Governments of India and Nepal, but to strengthen and improve them, so that we may realize all those expectations which the association

> with such a power like that of England naturally raises in our mind. I am fully conscious that our interests can best be served by the continuance of friendly relations between India and Nepal.[12]

Thus, Chandra Shumshere gave the British Government every facility in raising new Gurkha Battalions. In 1901 the Indian Army was remodelled on a more rational basis, which also effected the nature and status of the Gurkha Regiments. The original five Gurkha Regiments thus became the 1st to 5th Gurkha Rifles, and the next five places were occupied by the newer one. Thus the 9th Regiment of Bengal Infantry and the 10th Regiment of Madras Infantry became the 9th and 10th Gurkha Rifles respectively, while the other intervening places were occupied in 1903 by 42nd, 43rd and 44th Regiments as the 6th, 7th and 8th Gurkha Rifles respectively. Hence the process of remodelling the Gurkha Regiments which started in 1901 resulted in the formation of the Brigade of Gurkhas in 1903. The importance of the Gurkha Regi ments within the Indian Army was also recognised by the awarding of special honorifics, thus in 1906 the 1st Gurkha Rifles (Malaun Regiment) became the 1st Prince of wales Own Gurkha Rifles and in 1910 the 1st King George's Own Gurkha Rifles; in 1906 the 2nd Gurkha Rifles (Sirmoor Rifles) became the 2nd King Edward's Own Gurkha Rifles; and the 3rd Gurkha Rifles in 1907 became the 3rd The Queen's Own Gukrha Rifles and in 1908 the 3rd Queen Alexandra's Own Gurkha Rifles.[13] In 1906 Lord Kitchner, the Commander- in-Chief in India, paid a visit to Kathmandu, who developed close personal friendship with Chandra Shumshere. The title of the Honorary Colonel of the 4th Gurkha Rifles was offered to Chandra Shumshere. During his visit to England in 1908, Chandra Shumshere was presented with the G.C.B. (Grand Cross of the Order of Bath), by King Edward. As the mark of friendly relations between Nepal and Great Britain, the new King-Emperor George V visited Nepal's Terai for shooting in 1911.

In 1905, 71st Coorg Regiment and 76 Carnative Clite infantry was replaced by two new battalions of Gurkha, one of the Khas Gurkhas and other of the Gurungs and Magars. Chandra Shumshere who got all the possible incentives from the British changed every refusal of Bir Shumshere into a humble acceptance. He allowed 1800 Gurkha reservists to live in Nepal which in 1893 Bir Shumshere had refused. He also gave approval to the British plan of adding 2nd Battalions to all the ten Regiments of the Brigade of Gurkhas. Thus by 1908 the Gurkha Brigade had reached its perma nent establishment of 20 battalions organised into 10 rifle Regiments.[14] Upto 1914 the number of recruits required annually to maintain the 20 Gurkha battalions at full strength was 1500, strong which Nepal Darbar could easily provide. In 1914 there were some 26,000 Gurkhas serving in the 10 Rifle Regiments that formed the Brigade of Gurkhas of the Indian Army and the century long British anxiety on the question of the supply of Gurkha recruits from Nepal ended once and for all.

References

1. *Roberts Papers,* 4 September, 1891.
2. *Wylie to Sir Mortimer Duran*, dated Camp Via Segoulie, December 14, 1893 (Confidential) *Foreign Secret- E,* November 1896, Nos. 127-62 (N.A.I.).
3. *Foreign Department Secret-E*, February 1892, nos. 315-20, (N.A.I.).
4. *Ibid.*
5. Eden Vansittart, *Gurkhas: Hand book for the Indian Army, Op. Cit.*, pp. 174-75.
6. *Foreign Secret-E*, June, 1892, no. 136.
7. *Lord Roberts of Kandahar, Forty-one years in India.* Vol. II, Richard Bentlgy and Son, 1897, p. 452.
8. K. Mazundar, *Political Relations Between India and Nepal,* p. 62.

9. *Ibid.*

10. *Translation of a Yaddasht from the Prime Minister and Commander- in-Chief of Nepal, to the Resident in Nepal, no.261/50-71,* dated 29th Bhadon Sumvat, 1950 (September 24, 1893), received September 25, 1893, (N.A.I.).

11. *Foreign Department Secret-E*, July 1990, Nos. 284-85, (N.A.I.).

12. Percival Landon, *Nepal,* vol. II, p.108.

13. Christopher Chant, *Op. Cit.*, p. 68.

14. Sushila Tyagi, *Op. Cit*., p.211.

Surrender

CHAPTER SEVEN

Chandra Shumshere's positive attitude surpassed all limits during the Great War of 1914. Nepal's military aid started even before the British were practically fighting a decisive war. On August 3, 1914 Maharaja Chandra Shumshere handed over a very crucial letter to the Resident which contained the declaration of Chandra Shumshere's promise of loyalty to the British in the impending war. The letter was to be communicated to the Viceroy of India:

> The war cloud looks very threatening. In the event of a continental war Great Britain will in all probability be involved. I have come to request you to inform His Majesty the King Emperor that the whole military resources of Nepal are at His Majesty's disposal. We shall be proud if we can be of any service however little that may be. Though far from the scene of actual conflict we yield to none in our devotion and friendship to His Majesty's person and Empire. We have spoken of our friendship on many occasions. Should time allow, we hope to speak in deeds.
>
> I may say I am speaking in the double capacity, firstly as the Marshal of the Gurkhas and secondly as Major-General in His Majesty's Army.[1]

The above quoted letter shows the Prime Minister's deep rooted faith in furthering a noble relation with the British Army. Without getting involved in the notion of the actual strength of the Ally, he sacrificed his lot without a bargain. Since the British expeditionary forces sent to France were small in comparison to the heavy casualties, and since by the end of 1914 the British regular Army had been largely destroyed, the proposal of Chandra Shumshere was welcomed. Moreover, the need for the Nepalese help became more inevitable with the possibility of a German-Turkish invasion in India in alliance with Afgans. However, Chandra Shumshere's assistance did not remain limited in defending India from the German-Turkish invasion; Chandra Shumshere sent thousands of Gurkha soldiers across the ocean to participate in the actual operations of the World War. Thus, the Nepalese Government not just supplied the recruits and loaned the Nepalese troops along with offering the help in maintaining the British Gurkha Regiments, it also provided material and financial help and promised the Indian Government of keeping it informed about any intrigue against it from within.

With the outbreak of the War Chandra Shumshere took several steps to meet the British demand for recruits. Several persuasive methods were opted to induce recruits. Officers were specially appointed to take special precautions in recruiting fit and willing soldiers. Six recruit collecting centres were opened at Ilam, Dhankuta, Pokhara, Palpa, Sanjya and Doti in the first year of the war.[2] It was increased to ten in the subsequent year with a view to facilitate the collection of men at points near their homes. It was also said that those who served the British during the war would be considered to have been in service of their own country. The valley of Nepal and its adjoining districts where recruiting was normally prohibited were also opened for new recruit-yields. To induce volunteers a substantial allowance was granted to meet the cost of journey and other expenses. Cash money was given to the recruits-collecting locals. The Headman of the village was offered money and other rewards if he helped in finding the recruits. The result of the strong exertation of Maharaja and his officials was rich. During the entire period of the war, two lakhs fit soldiers were recruited.[3] He did not show any hesitation even in granting permission for opening a temporary recruiting depot at Kathmandu itself.

This was the period when Chandra Shumshere did not deny any of the British requests. His extremely co-operative attitude can be seen in his brief reply to Resident Manner Smith's following request:

> I have been asked to ascertain whether the following proposals for the continuance for Gurkha recruiting throughout the rainy season will meet your Excellency's approval:
>
> 1. The temporary depot at Kathmandu to be closed down.
> 2. Three Gurkha Officers and 100 selected non-commissioned officers and men to be kept in the recruiting districts of Nepal on recruiting duty with instructions to collect recruits and return to Gorukpore early in September.
> 3. Darjeeling depot to be kept open to carry on recruiting Districts of Nepal during rain.
>
> I Presume that I may get reply in the affirmative.[4]

To this Chandra Shumshere replied: "I write to inform you that they are approved".[5]

In order to please the British, Chandra Shumshere not only offered prisoners for Army service but also loaned the regular Nepalese troops to the British Government of India.In February 1915 British demand for 6000 Nepalese troops was immediately met. On 3rd and 4th March under General Babar Shumshere some 7501 men were sent to India.[6] The second contingent of 4000 troops was sent to India in December 1915. A third contingent was sent to India under the command of General Kaisher Shumshere and fourth contingent was sent under the command of the half brother of the Prime Minister, Maj General Sher

Shumshere.[7] Altogahter during this war Nepal Government loaned a total of about 16000 regular Nepalese troops to the British Government.[8]

Nepal's keen interest in keeping the British Gurkha Regiment upto strength can be seen in the efficiency with which Chandra Shumshere dealt with the soldiers of the Gurkha Regiment on leave. Since war had broken and it was important to recall the soldiers on leave at once, Chandra Shumshere sent special messengers to each village to make clear the urgency of the situation. He even threatened that those who failed to answer the call of war would be dealt with strictly. He made sure that no Gurkha sepoy was delayed because of any legal proceedings, because of non-payment of taxes or because of other family problems. Using his influence Chandra Shumshere also granted Patia[9] to the soldiers who went overseas.

The soldiers were promised that if they obtained a certificate from the British officers showing that they observed all the rites and rituals of caste and religion during their stay overseas, they will not face the threat of excommunication.[10]

Chandra Shumshere's desire to help did not remain confined to military aid only. On several occasions, he offered material and financial help on large scale. Though the first financial contribution of Rs.3,00,000/- was rejected in September 1914, on new year day of 1916 and again in January 1917 the amount of Rs.3,00,000/- presented to the Viceroy for military use were accepted. Then again in 1918, Rs. 2,00,000/- were presented. In addition to this cash contribution, 5000 Munds of Chandamous 84699 Pounds of Feal 200 jackets 12 great coats were sent to the soldiers.[11] 200000 broad gauge slifrers free of Royalty and 220 Sisoo logs were also supplied free of cost for the railways.[12] Nepal also presented 30 Machine Guns to the King Emperor in 1915.[13] Same year 340 mechanics from the Nepal Government's arms factories were offered to repair broken arms and to work in the Indian workshops. Out of 340 the services of 71 were accepted.[14]

Another important item of Nepal's contribution was Indian Rupees and Nepalese silver coins. Nepal managed to sent to Indian one crore and one lakh of British Indian Rupees and 25 lakh of Nepalese coins from the Government treasury.

Thus, during the First World War the country was thoroughly exploited after a brutal and brisk recruiting to maintain the British Indian Army. A dearth of manpower began and task of recruitment became more and more difficult. In the fourth year of War the depleted area of human population was once more mercilessly tried and considerable number of recruits were obtained. Even non-fighting classes were tried without a success. During First World War total number of men taken out of Nepal were 200000. One in ten never returned. Out of 200000 men, 55,000 men were enlisted in the regular Gurkha battalions of British Indian Army. Due to the tremendous efforts made by Chandara Shumshere in supplying the recruits, the British Government not only fulfilled the heavy loss in the regular Gurkha battalion but also raised many new battalions. In addition to this, a total of 16554 Gurkha soldiers from Nepalese Army were loaned for Garrison duties. During this war Nepal suffered some 20,000 casualties.[15] At the end of the war in 1918, the Government of India proposed the following rewards for the consideration of the British Government:

1. the status of Nepal might be so raised as to differentiate it unmistakably from the Indian Native States;
2. 'His Majesty' might be recognized as the title of the Maharajadhiraj;
3. the Prime Minister might be addressed as 'His Highness' instead of 'His Excellency';

Gurkha infantrymen in Hong Kong.

Men of the 1/10 Gurkha rifles capture an Indonesian parachutist in Malaya during the confrontation.

Men of the 2nd Gurkhas manning a three-inch mortar, Arakan 1944

4. the Prime Minister or his representative when visiting India on a mission, from the Nepal Government, might be given the title of 'Ambassador in place of that of 'Envoy';
5. some additional territory might be given to Nepal on the Philibit border or elsewhere, or some land might be given in perpetuity to the Prime Minister;
6. facilities might be offered to the Nepal Government for purchasing and importing cannons, rifles, ammunition, and warlike stores;
7. a gift of magazine rifles and ammunition might be made to the contingent of the Nepalese army when they returned from India to Nepal;
8. a gift of machine guns with ammunition might be made to the Prime Minister (for his personal protection) at the conclusion of the war or as soon as the guns could be spared.[16]

By the end of 1923 all but one of these recommendations were accepted. In place of additional territory, a grant of 10 lakh rupees per annum was granted.[17] In addition to this, Chandra Shumshere received almost all British titles. But the crowning achievement of Chandra Shumshere's diplomacy was the Treaty of Friendship 1923. By this treaty British Government granted the final confirmation of the full independent status of Nepal.

Gurkha recruitment went on satisfactorily between the two World Wars. The war clouds had already surrounded the European horizon by Octorber 1938. As soon as the War became a threat to Britain, Maharaja Judha Shumshere offered a Nepalese contingent of 8,000 troops for garrison duty in India. This offer was accepted a year later when War was actually declared. The British Government also asked for permission for Gurkhas to serve overseas, which Judha Shumshere readily granted. Permission was also given to enlist additional Gurkha for garrision, police duties and volunteer battalion of paratroopers. Judha Shumshere like his predecessors left no stone unturned to please the British authorities by supplying the adequate number of recruits. In all some 160,000 Gurkha recruits reported to the different recruiting centres.[18] Furthermore in early 1940 Maharaja Judha Shumshere sent Eight battalions of the Nepalese Army, commanded by two of his sons, to India, mostly destined for service on the frontier as before to release regular troops.

In the middle of 1940 the British Government sought permission to recruit 7000 Gurkhas for the 6 new Battalions during the recruiting season 1940-41. This figure however did not include the 3500 recruits required annually to maintain the existing Gurkha Regiments.[19] Maharaja Judha Shumshere readily granted his permis sion. When the first batch of the recruits were just reporting at the recruiting depots, the British Government made another urgent demand by asking permission to raise ten more Gurkha Battalions by April 1941.[20] Judha Shumshere gave his approval to these new proposals also. During the recruiting season of 1940, altogether 15,000 Gurkhas were recruited.[21] In order to supply required number of recruits to British Government, Judha Shumshere even stopped all recruitments for the Nepalese Army. During these years the recruitment had been so heavy that almost all the ablebodied youngmen had left the country and Nepalese Prime Minister delighted by the magnitude of his success in supplying the recruits wrote to the Indian Commander-in-Chief, A.P. Wavell;

> Bent on putting up what help we can to our great friend and ally in time of need my sole endeavour have remained directed to see the demand of recruits to the Indian army in full. It is a matter of gratification that the endeavour has proved successfull. For a small hill country like ours the supply of 65,000 recruits in the course of last three years is certainly a notable achievement.[22]

The supply of 65,000 recruits was only possible by opening new areas for recruitment which had been hitherto prohibited. The target for Gurkha recruitment for the year 1944-45 was 12,000. Maharaja Judha Shumshere who cautioned the British authorities about the quality of the recruits due to the heavy recruitments, left no stone unturned to meet the target.[23] All the ten Regiments of the Gurkha Brigade doubled their strength by raising third and fourth battalions whereas 1st, 2nd and 9th Gurkhas raised fifth Battalion also. In 1943 special battalions were formed as training battalions to give reruits realistic experience of combat and two Gurkha garrison units were also added. It has been estimated that by the end of the Second World War, the Gurkha serving with the British Indian Army was equivalent of some 55 battalions.[24] The cost to Nepal in dead alone was estimated to more than 10,000 men.

The wide and varied deployment of the Gurkhas clearly illustrates the extent of their overseas commitments; with the 1st Gurkhas operational in Burma, the 2nd Gurkhas widely used in Burma, Persia, the Western desert, Italy, Greece and Malaya, the 3rd, 4th and 5th Gurkhas had battalions in Burma and Italy, 6th Gurkhas served in Burma, Persia, Iraq, Palestine and Italy, the 1/7th Gurkhas fought in Burma where as 2/7 was captured in North Africa, was reconstituted and new one was serving in Syria, Lebanon, Palestine and Italy, the 8th and 9th Gurkhas had their battalion in Burma and Italy and the 10th Gurkhas served in Syria, Iraq, Italy, Palestine and Burma.[25] Judha Shumshere's co- operation to the British Government during the Second World War is evident from his letter dated March 11, 1945 to General Sir Claude Auchinleck, Commander-in-Chief of the Indian Army.

> It was indeed a great pleasure to receive your Excellency's kind letter No 50670/Rt.g. I (a) (2) dated 22nd February 1945 and to learn therefrom that the demand of 12,000 Gurkha recruits required during 1944-45 season has already been met in full. I suppose I need hardly write to tell your Excellency how deeply gratified I was at the news that my earnest efforts

to make the recruits available this time also had been crowned with success. What little wealth Nepal has is in her manpower, with that she has readily come forward as ever to the help of her great friend and ally during this war and her sons have not failed to show to the world of what stuff they are made. The fact that of the 20 Victoria crosses awarded to the Indian Army during this war 9 have been won by the Gurkha Brigade goes to prove it without doubt. Rifles having won 3 V.C. created a record and it deserves our hearty congratulation on it.

The information that during the 1945-46 recruiting season Your Excellency would not require more than 5,000 recruits to maintain the Gurkha units has been noted. Every effort will of course be made to make that number available when the time for that comes. Heavily recruited as the country has been during the last 5 years I am afraid the quality of the recruits that would then be available would be rather poorer. In our army too we are feeling the pinch and recourse has had to be taken to fill up vacan cies with recruits of lower standard and that too with much difficulty.[26]

The Gurkha recruitment which initially started with smuggling of recruits reached to an anti-climax in 1945 when Indian Commander-in-Chief proposed to reduce the number. In a letter to the Nepalese Prime Minister Judha Shumshere, he wrote:

It is with greatest pleasure that I am now able to inform Your Highness that, as a result of further detailed examination of the manpower situation I am in a position to reduce my demand for Gurkha recruits for the year 1945-46 to 2,000 only. This will be ample to maintain existing Gurkha Rifle Regiments at full strength.[27]

References

1. *Letter from Chandra Shumshere to the Resident* September 1914, *Foreign Ministry Nepal,* Poka No.63.

2. *Ibid.*

3. David Bolt, *Op. Cit.*, p.90.

4. *Manner-Smith to Chandra Shumshere*, July 1, 1915, *Foreign Ministry Nepal,* Poka No. 66-B.
5. *Ibid.,* July 5, 1915.
6. *Ibid.,* Poka no. 51.
7. *Ibid.*
8. *Ibid.*
9. *Patia*. Permission given by the Brahmin priest to go overseas and upon their return to be accepted in Hindu society without any religious penalty after performing a certain religious ceremony.
10. *Foreign Ministry Nepal,* Poka No. 63.
11. *Ibid.*
12. *Ibid.*
13. *Ibid.*, Poka No.64.
14. Ibid.
15. David Bolt, *Op. Cit.,* p.90.
16. *Foreign and Political Department Secret Internal Proceedings, July* 1919, Nos. 36-65 (N.A.I.).
17. Resident to Maharaja October 16, 1919, *Foreign Ministry Nepal,* Register No. 1.
18. David Bolt, p. 98.
19. *Letter from Betham to the Maharaja Joodha* June 15, 1940, *Foreign Ministry Nepal,* Poka No.560.
20. *Ibid.* September 15, 1940.
21. *Ibid.*
22. Letter from Maharaja Joodha to General A.P. Wavell, Commander-in-Chief of India, February 25, 1943, *Foreign Ministry Nepal,* Fill No.17.
23. *Ibid.* September 21, 1944, Fill No. 42.
24. Chritopher Chant, *Op. Cit.,* p.101.
25. *Ibid.* p.105.

26. Juddha to General Sir Calude Auchinleck Commander-in-Chief of India March 11, 1945, *Foreign Ministry Nepal,* Poka No.56.

27. General Sir Claude Auchinleck to Maharaja Juddha Shumshere June 30, 1945, *Ibid*.

Myth

CHAPTER EIGHT

With the end of the War all the war-raised Gurkha Battalions were disbanded. The proposal for the Indian Independence in the post- War era necessiated the reorganisation of the Gurkha Regiments for this, a tripartite agreement was concluded in August 1947 between the British, the Indian and the Nepalese Government. This agreement confirmed that four of the Gurkha Regiments would go to the British Army and that the other six would remain part of the Indian Army. It was also agreed that the Gurkha Regiments should not be used against Nepal, other Gurkhas and Hindus or unarmed mobs. The eight Battalions of the 2nd, 6th, 7th and 10th Gurkha Rifles which under the British Army, formed the new Brigade of Gurkhas left India for their new destination in Malaya at the beginning of 1948.[1] But the recruitment for these battalions was agreed to be done in recruiting depots in India. When the Indian Government imposed ban on these recruitments on Indian soil, the British Government, therefore, entered into an agreement with Nepal in July 1953. This agreement which permitted the British to open recruiting depots at Dharam and Paklihawa was subject to renewal every five years. In 1958 this agreement was extended for another ten years.[2]

The Brigade of Gurkhas was made self-reliant by the addition of separate units of Gurkha Engineers, Gurkha

Singhals and Gurkha Transport Regiment. The status of the infantry regiments was also enhanced when 6th Gurkhas became the 6th Queen Elizabeth's Own Gurkha Rifles, the 7th Gurkhas became the 7th Duke of Edinburgh's Own Gurkha Rifles and 10th Gurkhas became the 10th Princes Mary's Own Gurkha Rifles.[3] The British policy of gradual withdrawal from the far east resulted in the reduction of the strength of the Gurkha Regiments. The shrinking of the Brigade of Gurkhas which started in 1963 ended only in 1971 when the conservative Government in England halted the rundown of the Gurkhas. By this time there remained only five battalions of Gurkhas with a total strength of 7000 men. The 2nd Gurkhas was the only two battalion regiment. In 1975 another cut was ordered by which the Gurkhas were to be reduced to 6,000 men by 1979. But in 1982 the Brigade of Gurkhas was ordered to be augumented and 2nd battalions was added to the 7th Gurkhas.[4]

The Gurkhas under the British flag saw action in Malaya, the Indonesian confrontation, troubles in Borneo and Brunei, the Cypriot War and Britain's War with Argentina in 1982 for the Falkland Islands.

Currently four battalions, with the headquarters of the Brigade of Gurkhas, are stationed in Hong Kong, together with The Queen's Gurkha Engineers. The Queen's Gurkha Singnals and the Gurkha Transport Regiment. The fifth Battalion is regularly located in England and the Sixth battalion in Brunei.

For almost 176 years the Gurkha Brigade of the British Army have been the stuff of song and legend. Since its inception in 1815 the Gurkha soldiers of the British Gurkha Battalions, with their famous Khukri have proved themselves as the finest warriors in the world. Sir Ralph Turner, a British Gurkha officer wrote during the first world war, that the Gurkhas were the bravest of the brave, indomitable, uncomplaining, unwavering and most faithful friends.[5] In the 1982 Falkland's war the role of the Gurkha soldiers was highly publi cized, when welding their Khukris, they forced the surrender of two companies of Argentine troops.

The British Government's decision to return Hong Kong to China in 1997 had raised some doubt about the future of the Brigade of Gurkhas.

The changed political context in Nepal has generated hot discussions on the very concept of allowing the country's youths to join the foreign armies. The critics argue that regular and unhindered recruitment by the British and Indian armies is stripping Nepal of some of its brightest young men, whose talents might be used in building up the homeland. They argue that the Nepalese youths in foreign armies fighting the wars against the countries which has no enmity with Nepal, is not a right thing. They point out that the Gurkha units in the Indian army have fought against China and Pakistan and more recently they were sent to Sri Lanka as part of an Indian peace keeping force, although Nepal does not want to autagonize any of those countries. The involvement of Gurkha troops in the 1982 Falklands war also had raised some controversy in the diplomatic circles. According to them this practice is not only against the national prestige of Nepal but also a potential source of diplomatic embarrassment. "Export of mercenaries" as they say, must be stoped immediately.

On the other hand the supporters of continued recruitment assert that if all the soldiers are brought home a serious problem of unemployment is inevitable. Moreover the country is getting nearly 47 million dollars annually as foreign exchange from British Gurkhas as salary, remittances and pensions and Indian currency worth 100 million dollars from those in Indian army. There is no doubt that the economic aspect of the Gurkha recruitment not only provides the nation with precious foreign exchange but also serves as the lifeline for the many hill people for whom, joining foreign army is the major wayout to make a better living for themselves and their families.

The British Government on June 4,1991 announced its decision to cut down its army strength by 25 percent. With this, the speculations were made that the entire Brigade of Gurkha will be disbanded. This news came as a shock not only to the families and relatives of those Gurkha soldiers who are serving under the British flag, but also to those aspirant Nepalese youths who are planning to join that army. After much speculation and guess work the British government finally announced its decision on the Brigade of Gurkhas. The Brigade is to stay but the number is to be reduced from present 8,000 men to a strength of 2500 men only.

References

1. Christopher Chant, *Op. Cit.*, p. 146.
2. Grishma Bahadur Devkota, *Nepal ko Rajnaitik Darpan,* Kathmandu, 2036, p.171.
3. Christopher Chant, *Op. Cit.* p.151.
4. Byron Farwell, *Op. Cit.*, p.277.
5. *Time*,the weekly newsmagazine, vol. 138, No.4, July 29, 1991, p.9.

Appendices

APPENDIX I

CONVENTION or Agreement entered into between Kajee Ummer Sing Thappa and Major - General Ochterlony, on the 15th May 1815

In consideration of the high rank and character of Kajee Ummer Sing Thappa, and of the skill, bravery, and fidelity with which he has defended the country committed to his charge, it is agreed:

1. That Kajee Ummer Sing Thappa, with the troops now in Raujgurh, shall march out and retain their arms and accoutrements, the colours of their respective corps, two guns and all private property, which shall be duly respected and preserved, and every attention and delicacy observed in respect to the Zenana of the Kajee, and every person under his authority.

2. In consideration, also, of the gallant conduct of Kajee Runjore Sing Thappa, it is agreed that he shall likewise march out of the fort of Jeytuck with two hundred men, who are to retain their arms, colours, and one gun, with the Bharadara (chief officers) and their followers, about three hundred more in number, unarmed, with his own and their private property, which shall be respect ed, and the sanctity of the Zenana preserved.

3. Kajee Ummer Sing Thappa and Kajee Runjore Sing Thappa, with their property and followers, are at liberty to proceed by the route of Thaneisur, Hurdwar and Nujeebabad, to join the troops eastward of the river Surjoo, or by which ever route they determine to proceed to that destination. Conveyance

shall be provided for the transportation of their property to the confines of the Nepaul territory.

4. Kajee Ummer Sing Thappa and Kajee Runjore Sing Thappa, shall be at liberty to meet wherever they please.

5. All the troops in the service of Nepaul, with the exception of those granted to the personal honour of the Kajees, Ummer Sing and Runjore Sing, will be at liberty to enter into the service of the British Government, if it is agreeable to themselves and the British Government choose to accept their services, and those who are not employed will be maintained on a specific allowance by the British Government, till peace is concluded between the two States.

6. Kajee Ummer Sing Thappa, on his part, agrees to leave the fort of Malown, whenever bearers and other conveyance are prepared for his private property.

7. Kajee Ummer Sing Thappa also agrees to send immediate orders for the evacuation and delivery, to persons properly authorized, of the forts of Bhylee (Irkee), Subbatoo, Mornee, Jeytuck, Juggutgurh, Rowaheen, and all other forts and fortresses now held by the Nepaul troops between the Jumna and Sutleje rivers. The garrisons of all which forts, strong holds, &c shall enjoy their private property unmolested, and the arms and warlike stores in each shall be left in deposit, for the future decision of the Right Honourable the Governor-General; with exception to such among them as are related to Kajee Ummer Sing Thappa by kindred, about eighty-three men, who shall be at liberty to retain their arms and accoutrements.

8. Kajee Ummer Sing Thappa also agrees to send immediate orders to Kajee Bukhtour Sing for the evacuation of the territory of Ghurwall, to deliver over the forts, &c in that district to the officers of the British Government, and to proceed to Nepaul by the Kamaon route, with their garrisons, all public and property including warlike stores, accompanied by a chuprassie with a pass, on the part of the British Government.

Separate Article – Kajee Ummer Sing Thappa wishes it to be understood, that he shall give immediate orders for the in stant surrender of the distant forts, in the hope that it may lead to an early renewal of the relations of amity which have subsisted between the two states for these sixty years, and by the advice of Bum Sah and the Bharadars of Kamaon.

APPENDIX II

Copy of the letter from the Secretary to the Government of India to the Honourable Edward Gardner Commissioner of Kumaon, authorising him, for the formation of a provincial troop of Gurkhas.

Tuttyghar,
Dated, 11th June, 1815

From The Secretary to Government

To The Hon'bld Edward Gardner
Commissioner of Kumaon

Sir,

I have the honour to acknowledge the receipt of your despatch dated the 1st instant.

Adverting to the considerations in the last paragraph of that despatch, the Governor-General is pleased to authorise you to entertain as provincial troops for service in the Hills, a proportion of Gorkhas, or Nipalese, especially such as have families resident in Kumaun and Garhwal, with regard to the number to be admitted into out service, you will please consult the commanding officers in Kumaun, by whose opinion jointly with your own the decision must be guided.

I have the honour to be, sir,

Your most obedient servant
Sd/-......J. Adam.......
Secretary to the Government

APPENDIX III

Progressive Title Changes of the Gurkha Regiments

Ist King George V's Own Gurkha Rifles (the Malaun Regiment):

1815 Ist Nasiri Battalion; 1823 5th, 6th or Ist Nasiri Local Battalion; 1843 4th or Nasiri (Rifle Battalion); 1850 66th or Goorkha Regiment, Bengal Native Infantry; 1988 66th or Goorkha Light Infantry Regiment, Bengal Native Infantry; 1861 11 Regiment of Bengal Native Infantry; 1861 Ist Goorkha Regiment (Light Infantry); 1891, Ist Gurkha (Riflle) Regiment; 1901 Ist Gurkha Rifles; 1903 Ist Gurkha Rifle (the Malaun Regiment); 1906 Ist Prince of Wales's Own Gurkha Rifles; 1910 Ist King George's Own Gurkha Rifles (The Malaun Regiment); 1937 Ist King George V's Own Gurkha Rifles (the Malaun Regiment); 1947 left the British service.

2nd King Edward VII's Own Goorkhas (the Sirmoor Rifles):

1815 Sirmoor Battalion; 1823 8th (or Sirmoor) Local Battalion; 1886 6th (or Sirmoor) Local Battalion; 1850 Sirmoor Battalion; 1858 Sirmoor Rifle Regiment; 1861 7th Regiment of Bengal Native Infantry; 1861 2nd Goorkha Regiment; 1864 2nd Goorkha (the Sirmoor Rifles) Regiment; 1876 and (Prince of Wales's Own) Goorkha Regiment (the Sirmoor) Rifles; 1886 2nd (the Prince of Wales's Own) Goorkha Regiment (The Sirmoor Rifles); 1891 2nd (the prince of wales's Own) Gurkha (Rifles) Regiment (the Sirmoor Rifles); 1901 2nd (the Prince of Wales's Own) Gurkha Rifles (the Sirmoor Rifles) ; Ist January 1906 2nd King Edward's VII's Own Goorkhas (the Sirmoor Rifles); 1947 to British Army.

3rd Queen Alexandra's Own Gurkha Rifles:

1815 Kumaon Battalion; 1816 Kumaon Provincial Battalion; 1823 9th (or Kumaon) Local Battalion; 1826 7th (or Kumaon) Local Battalion; 1860 Kumaon Battalion; 1861 18th Regiment of Bengal Native Infantry; 1861 3rd Goorkha Regiment; 1864 3rd (the Kumaon) Goorkha Regiment; 1887 3rd Goorkha Regiment; 1891 3rd Goorkha (Rifle) Regiment; 1901 3rd Gurkha Rifles; 1907 3rd The Queen's Own Gurkha Rifles; 1908 3rd Queen Alexandra's Own Gurkha Rifles; 1947 left the British Service.

4th Prince of Wales's Own Gurkha Rifles:

1857 Extra Goorkha Regiment; 1861 19th Regiment of Bengal Native Infantry; 1861 4th Goorkha Regiment; 1891 4th Gurkha (Rifle) Regiment; 1901 4th Gurkha Rifles; 1924 4th Prince of Wales's Own Gurkha Rifles, 1947 left the British service.

5th Royal Gurkha Rifles (Frontier Force):

1858 25th Punjab Infantry, or Hazara Goorkha Battalion; 1861 7th Regiment of Infantry (or Hazara Goorkha Battalion), Punjab Irregular Force; 1861 5th Goorkha Regiment, or Hazara Goorkha Battalion; 1886 5th Goorkha Regiment, the Hazara Goorkha Battalion; 1887 5th Goorkha Regiment; 1891 5th Gurkha (Rifle) Regiment; 1901 5th Gurkha Rifles; 1903 5th Gurkha Rifles (Frontier Force); 1923 5th Royal Gurkha Rifles (Frontier Force); 1947 left the British service.

6th Queen Elizabeth's Own Gurkha Rifles:

1817 Cuttack Region; 1823 Rangpur Light Infantry Battalion; 1826 8th (or Rangpur) Local Light Infantry Battalion; 1828 8th (or Assam) Local Light Infantry Battalion; 1844 Ist Assam Light Infantry; 1961 46th Regiment of Bengal Native Infantry; 1861 42nd Regiment of Bengal Native Infantry; 1864 12nd (Assam) Regiment of Bengal Native (Light) Infantry; 1885 42nd (Assam) Regiment of Bengal (Light) Infantry; 1886 42nd Regiment Goorkha Light Infantry; 1889 42nd (Goorkha) Regiment of Bengal (Light) Infan try; 1891 42nd Gurkha (Rifle) Regiment of Bengal Infantry; 1901 42nd Gurkha Rifles; 1903 6th Gurkha Rifles; 1947 to British Army, 1959 6th Queen Elizabeth's Own Gurkha Rifles.

7th Duke of Edinburgh's Own Gurkha Rifles:

1902 8th Gurkha Rifles; 1903 2nd Battalion, 10th Gurkha Rifles; 1907 7th Gurkha Rifles; 1947 to British Army; Ist January 1959 7th Duke of Edinburgh's Own Gurkha Rifles.

8th Gurkha Rifles:

1824 16th or Sylhet Local Battalion; 1826 11th or Sylhet Local (Light)Infantry Battalion; 1961 48th Regiment of Bengal Native Infantry; 1861 44th Regiment of Bengal Native Infantry; 1864 (Sylhet) 44th Regiment of Bengal Native (Light) Infantry; 1885 44th (Sylhet) Reginal of Bengal (Light) Infantry; 1886 44th (Sylhet) Regiment of

Bengal (Light) Infantry; 1886 44th Regi ment, Goorkha (Light) Infantry; 1889 44th (Goorkha) Regiment of Bengal (Light) Infantry; 1891 44th Gurkha (Rifle) Regiment of Bengal Infantry; 1901 44th Gurkha Rifles; 1903 3rd Gurkha Rifles; 1907 became the Ist Battalion, 2nd Battalion, raised at Gauhati; 1835 Assam Sebundy Corps; 1839 Lower Assam Sebundy Corps; 1839 Ist Assam Sebundy Corps; 1844 2nd Assam Light Infantry; 1861 47th Regiment of Bengal Native Infantry; 1861 43rd Regiment of Bengal Native Infantry; 1884 43rd (Assam) Regiment of Bengal Native (Light) Infantry; 1865 43rd (Assam) Regiment of Bengal (Light) Infantry; 1886 43rd Regiment Goorkha Light Infantry; 1889 43rd (Goorkha) Regiment of Bengal (Light) Infantry; 1891 43rd Gurkha (Rifle) Regiment of Bengal Infantry; 1901 43rd Gurkha Rifles; 1903 7th Gurkha Rifles; 1907 became the 2nd Battalion, 8th Gurkha Rifles; 1947 left the British Service.

9th Gurkha Rifles:

1817 Fatehgarh Levy; 1819 Manipuri Levy; 1823 Ist Battalion, 32nd Regiment of Bengal Native Infantry; 1824 63rd Regiment of Bengal Native Infantry; 1861 9th Regiment of Bengal Native Infantry; 1885 9th Regiment of Bengal Infantry; 1894 9th (Gurkha Rifles) Regiment of Bengal Infantry; 1903 9th Gurkha Rifles; 1947 left the British service.

10th Princess Mary's Own Gurkha Rifles:

1890 the Regiment of Burma Infantry; 1891 10th Regi ment (Ist Burma Battalion) of Madras Infantry; 1892 10th Regiment (Ist Burma Rifles) Madras Infantry; 1895 10th Regiment (Ist Burma Gurkha Rifles) Madras Infantry; 1901 10th Gurkha Rifles ; 1947 to British Army; 1949 10th Princess Mary's Own Gurkha Rifles.

Source : J.N.R. Nicholson, *The Gurkha Rifles,*
Berkshire 1974, Pp. 22-24.

APPENDIX IV

Darbar's Order to Kriti Bahadur Shah – Governor of Jhalhara
[8th June 1885]

As the British Government has asked the Darbar to allow to enlist, in the British Army, any Nepalese who are willing to do so, and as the British Government has furnished details as to the terms of service, therefore, such men in the villages in your jurisdiction as may agree to the said terms, and of their own will intend to serve the British Government, should present themselves in the nearest Militia Court in Nepal. Nobody is required by force to do so, nor is any one prohibited from so doing. We will be pleased with those who come to enlist, now, because by so doing the Darbar will consider them to be acting in a straight forward manner. But those who on now being asked do not agree to enlist, and afterwards go to enlist by stealth, will be considered guilty of deceit and punished.

Make the "Dowari Mookhias" (officials) of the various stations, under you understand fully the said terms, and orders them to enquire how many men in their jurisdiction are (or whether there is none) willing to go to enlist and to report the matter to you within nine days. You should then submit these reports throught the Goshwara Amini. Those who come to enlist willingly should be men from 18 to 27 years of age, they should not be of smaller statuee than 5 feet 3 inches, and should be 32 inches round chest. No distinction of caste is to be made. If the Mookhias and Dowaries (officials) of various villages submit reports now under their seal and signature, that there is nobody willing to enlist, and afterwards if it appears that any one goes to enlist within the next 3 years from any lakhs, it will be Dowaries concerned will be brought to punishment for neglect. A register is to be kept in which the names of men who willing come to the Militia Court to enlist, as wèll as their parentage and residence, should be recorded. This register should bear the scal of the Court, and should be sent up along with the recruits through the Jaisi Kotha Court to the Goshwara Court.

Those wo come willingly to enlist will get travelling expenses and service as detailed.

Source; *F.S.E.*, October 1885, No. 66.

APPENDIX V

Barkeley to Runodeep Singh (16th August 1886)

The extreme and unnecessary insistance and repititon of the fact (which every one knows) "that no man need enlist unless he is willing". That "nobody is required to enlist by force" are surely more likely to raise doubt and dread than to encourage men to enlist.

Again, the threat that persons enlisting in future will be punished (though its objects, I understand from the orderly officers, to induce a great number of men to enlist at once) is clearly not in accordance with the understanding that all restrictions on recruiting were to be entirely removed...the instructions given to the local officials to enquire how many men in their jurisdiction are willing to enlist. "For whether there are none' are, I think, calculated to convey an erroneous impression.

Source: *F.S.E.*, October, 1885, No. 67.

APPENDIX VI

Order of Prime Minister (24th August 1885)

Whereas the British Government wishes to obtain subjects of the Nepalese Government as securities for service in the British Army, the Nepalese Government – desiring to show its friendship for the British Government – hereby notifies that it's you (i.e. the Nepalese subjects) wish to enlist in the British army, you should present yourself to the nearest nepalese offi cers, from whom you will learn all particulars as to the terms of pay, service, and pension etc. There is full permission from my government to enlist in the British service, and there is no re striction whatever about it.

The Nepalese Government will be pleased with those who go to enlist. The persons going to enlist should present them selves to the British recruiting agents on the frontier.

Source: *F.S.E.,* October, 1885, No. 70.

APPENDIX VII

Telegram from Resident to Foreign Secretary (28 December 1885)

Several young and excellent men have volunteered with sanction of Darbar from Nepal regiments for our service. Should they be accepted?

Source: *F.S.E.*, January, 1885, No. 102.

Telegram from Foreign Secretary to Resident (31st December 1885)

Your telegram of 28th Gurkha recruits. No objection. It is presumed that men are Gurkhas of the proper classes.

Source: F.S.E., January, 1886, No. 103.

APPENDIX VIII

1907 पौष वदी 4 रजि 2 मा वम वहादुर ले जंग वहादुर लेखेको पत्रः-

"इ सवै मानिस लाइ रजिडेन्ट साहेब छेऊ पु-याइ देऊ साहेव वाट वुझाउंदा सम्झाउदा भान्दछ्न भामन्या भर्ती हवन ताहा भर्ती भएनन भन्या यहां पजनी सकियो विदा गरी पढाई विन्छू भन्या कुरा गर्नु भनी कप्तान शम्शेर जंग खत्री, अमीर मुन्सी, ज्यादार महावीर खत्री इ तिन जना लाइ रजिडन्टी कोठीमा पठाउदा ती दुइ हजार जति मानिस लाइ णड गरी हाप्रो वोली सम्झन्या छैनन तिमिहरू को वोली ले को राजी हुंछौ अनी सोध भन्या कुरा गया छ्न र हाम्रा कप्तान मुन्सीले सोदा जांन्छी भन्या कोही भयनन 2 जना मानिस जान्छौ भन्या उस्मा येक जना लठुमांग्रा दुवलो अर्को एक जना निहाट्टा पुडको णडा हुंदा इंच मा मिल्दैन हुदैन भनी साहेव ले भन्याछ्न......"।

APPENDIX IX

सम्वत 1914 सालमा जंगबहादुरले सुदुर पश्चिम नेपालका जिल्लाधिश में. ज. कृष्ण ध्वजलाई पठाएको निर्देशन :-

हाम्रा मुलुकका गोर्खाली मानिसहरू लाई अल्मोडा गइ पल्टनमा भर्ती नहुन भनी साहेवले थाहा नपाउन्या गरी उर्दी दिन। दुनियां लाइ कर लगाइ भर्ती गर्न भन्या हुदैन आफना कुसुले भर्ती हुन आउन्याहरू घाटमा रोकिन्या छैनन। णुनषत गरी जान्या मात्र रोकिन्या छ्त भनि निज साहेव लाइ लेखी पठाउन्या का गरौ।"

APPENDIX X

संवत 1942 साल भाद्र वदी 8 रजि 4 को दिन जारी भएको इस्तिहार :-

"आगे सर्कार नेपालका रैयत दुनिया प्रति वृटिश का फौज निमिन्त नेपाली रिकूटहरू पाउनको बृटिश सरकार इच्छा राणछ्न नेपाले सरकारवाट बृटिश सरकारलाई आफनो दोस्ति देणाउनको णतिरले यो इस्तेहार जारी भयो की तिमीहरू वृटिशका पल्टनमा भर्ति हुनको इच्छाउन्याले नगिचका हाम्रा नेपाली हाकिम छेउ हाजिर हुनु र मोसुफ हाकीम वाट यस्तो नोकरी येती तलव यती पेन्सेन पाउंछौं भंनया इत्यादि वेहोरा थाहा पाउन्या छौं। वृटिश सकारिको नोकरीमा भर्ति हुन जानालाई हाम्रा सर्कार वाट पुरा इजाजत छ कुनै तर्हको रोकावट छैन जाने हरू देखि सर्कार नेपाल णुसि हुन्या छन् ति जानेहरूले रीकूट ज्मा ग-र्या अफीसर सग हाजिर मै निजहरू ले दियाको उर्दी वर्माजिम गर्याकाम गर।

संवत 1968 देखि गोर्खा राइफल्सका जवानहरू लेपनि पान थाले। दूइ विश्व युद्ध मा 12 जनाले पाए। पे. 15

चिन्तरकजन नेपाली-नेपाल र बृटिश गोर्खा राइफल्स" रूपरेखा नेपाली मासिक काठमानू पशुपति प्रस वर्ष 5, अंक 4 पूणांक 40.

APPENDIX-XI

Gurkha VCs

	Name	Regiment	Place of action	Date of action	Gazetted in London Gazette.
1.	Rfm Kulbir Thapa	2/3rd GR	France	25 September 1915	18 November 1915
2.	Rfm Karnabhadur Rana	2/3rd GR	Egypt	10 April 1818	21 June 1918
3.	Subadar Lalbahadur Thapa	1/2nd GR	Tunisia	5/6 April 1943	15 June 1943
4.	Havildar Gaje Ghale	2/6th RGR	Burma	24-7 May 1944	30 September 1944
5.	Rfm Ganju Lama	1/7th GR	Burma	12June 1944	7 September 1944
6.	Rfm Tulbahadur Pun	3/6th GR	Burma	23 June 1944	9 November 1944
7.	Rfm Agansing Rai	5th RGR	Burma	24-5 June 1944	5 October 1944
8.	A/Subadar Netrabahadur Thapa	2/5 RGR	Burma	25-6 June 1944	12 October 1944,
9.	Rfm Sherbahadur Thapa	1/9th GR	Italy	18 September 1944	28 December 1944
10.	Rfm Thaman Gurung	1/5th RGR	Italy	19 November 1944	22 February 1945
11.	Rfm Bhanbagta Gurung	3/2nd GR	Burma	5 March 1945	5 June 1945
12.	Rfm Lachhiman Gurung	4/8th GR	Burma	12 May 1945	27 July 1945
13.	L/C Rambahadur Limbu	2/10th GR	Bonne	21 November 1965	22 April 1966

Selected Bibliography

Primary Sources

Foreign Ministry Nepal, Kathmandu

Nepal Government records, Documents, Secret correspondence, Yadhastha and records of the Conversations etc., kept in different *Pokas* (Bundles).

Royal Nepal Army-Headquarter, Kathmandu

Documents relating to the question of Gurkha Recruitment. Orders to the district officers and Istihars (Public orders) relating to the Gurkha recruitment.

National Archives India, New Delhi

1. Foreign Political Consultations. 2. Foreign Political Proceedings. 3. Foreign Political A. 4. Foreign Political B. 5. Foreign Secret Consultations. 6. Foreign Secret E. 7. Foreign Secret F. 8. Foreign Department Proceedings.

Printed Books

Aitchinson, C.U.,*A Collection of Treaties,* Engagements and Sanads Relating to India and Neighbouring Countries, Vol. XIV., New Delhi, Central Publishing Branch, 1929.

Bhandari, D.R., *Nepal Ko Aitihasik Vivechana,* Varanasi; Krishna Kumari, 1958.

Bhattacharjee, G.P., *India and Politics of Modern Nepal,* Calcutta; The Minerva Associates, 1970.

Bolt, David, *Gurkhas,* London: Weidenfeld and Nicolson, 1967.

Boulger, C.C., *England and Russia in Central Asia,* London, 1879.

Cavenagh, Orfeur; *Rough Notes on the state of Nepal, Its Government, Army and Resources;* Calcutta; W.Palmer, Military Orphan Press, 1851.

Chant, Christopher,*Gurkha,* England, Blandford Press, 1985.

Chaudhuri, K.C., *Anglo-Nepalese Relations, from the Earliest Times of the British rule in India till the Gurkha War,* Calcutta: Modern Book Agency, 1960.

Dabral, Shiva Prasad, *Uttarakhand Ka Itihas,* Part 5, Godha Garwal: Birgatha Prakashan, 2030 B.S.

Devkota, Grishma Bahadur, *Nepal Ko Rajnitik Darpan*, Kathmandu, 2036 B.S.

Farwell, Byron, *The Gurkhas,* Great Britain, Penguin Books, 1985.

Forbes, Ducan, *Johnny Gurkha,* London: Robert Hele, 1964.

Gimlette, G.H.D., *Nepal and the Nepalese,* London, H.F. and G Witherby, 1928.

Hunter, William Wilson, *Life of Brain Houghton Hodgson, British Resident at the Court of Nepal,* London; John Murray, 1896.

Husain, Asad, *British India's Relations with the Kingdom of Nepal (1857-1947)*, London, George Allen and Unwin Ltd., 1970.

Jackson, Donovan, *India's Army,* London; Sampson Low, Marston and Co: Ltd, n.d.

James, Harold and Shell Devis, *The Gurkhas,* London; Macdonald and Co. Ltd., 1965.

Karan, Pradhumna P. and Jenkins, William M., *The Himalayan Kingdoms,* Bhutan, Sikkim and Nepal, Newjersey, U.S.A., Van Nostrand and Company, Inc., Princeton, 1963.

Khanal, Yadu Nath, *Nepal Between India and China: An Aspect of the Evolving International Balance in Asia,* Massachussets: Harvard University, 1971.

Landon, Percival, *Nepal Vol. I!,* London; Constable and Company, 1928.

Macdonell, Ronald, and Macanley, Mercus, *A History of the 4th prince of Wales's Own Ghurkha Rifles 1857-1937,* Vol I., Edinburgh and London, William Blackwood and Sons Ltd., 1940.

Markham, C.R., *Mission of George Bogle to Tibet and of the Journey of Thomas Manning to Lahsa,* London, Toubner and Co., 1879.

Mojumdar K., *Anglo-Nepalese Relations in the Nineteenth Century,* Calcutta, Firma K.L. Mukhopadhya, 1973.

—— *Political Relations Between India and Nepal*, Pvt. Ltd., 1973.

Morris, C.J., *The Gurkhas, A Handbook for the Indian Army,* Delhi; Manager of Publications, 1933.

Nicholson, J.B.R., *The Gurkha Rifles,* Berkshire, Osprey Publishing Ltd., 1974.

Northey, W.B., *The Land of the Gurkhas, or the Himalayan Kingdom of Nepal,* Cambridge: W.Heffer, 1937.

Oldfield, Henry Ambrose, *Sketches from Nepal,* Vol.I, London; W.H. Allen, 1880.

Pemable, John, *The Invasion of Nepal*, John Company at War, London: Oxford Clarendon Press, 1971.

Ramakant, *Indo- Nepalese Relations, 1816 to 1877,* New Delhi, S. Chand, 1968.

—— *Nepal, China and India,* New Delhi; Abinav Publications, 1976.

Rose. Leo E., *Nepal Strategy for Survival,* Delhi Oxford University Press, 1973.

Shrestha, Sita, *Nepal and the United Nations,* New Delhi; Sindhu Publications Ltd., 1974.

Tuker, Sir Francis, *Gurkhas, The Story of the Gurkhas of Nepal,* London, Constable and Company Ltd., 1957.

Tyagi, Sushila, *Indo-Nepalese Relations (1858- 1914)*, Delhi, D.K. Publishing House, 1974.

Vansittart, Eden, *Gurkha, Handbook for the Indian Army,* Calcutta; Superintendent Government Printing, 1906.

Woodyatt, Nigel G., *The Regimental History of the 3rd Queen Alexandra's Own Gurkha Rifles 1815-1927*, London, Philip Allen & Co. Ltd., 1929.

Yogi, Narahari Nath and Acharya Baburam (ed.), Rastrapita Shri Panch Bada Maharaja Prithivi Narayan Shah Devko Dibya Upadesh, (Divine Counsel of father of the nation His Majesty King Prithivi

Narayan Shah Dev), Kathmandu, Prithivi Jayanti Samachar Samitti 1951.

Articles in Periodicals

Nepali, Chitaranjan, "Nepal Ra British Gurkha Rifles", *Roop Rekha*, Kathmandu, August, 1964.

Pandey, M.R., "Angrej Haruko Nepal Prati Bhavana, 1767-1814", *Voice of History*, Vol. I, Kathmandu, T.U. History Association, 1974.

Corporal Ram Bahadur Limbu who won the Vc in Sarawak in 1966.

Men of the 7th Gurkha Rifles mount guard at Buckingham Palace, December 1, 1971

Gurkha Vc's

Rifleman Ganju Lama
Burma, June 1944

Rifleman Tulbahadur Pun
Burma, June 1944

Rifleman Agamsing Rai
Burma, June 1944

Rifleman Kulbir Thapa,
France, 1915

Subedar Lalbahadur Thapa
N. Africa, April 1943

Haviladar Ganje Ghale
Burma, May 1944

Rifleman, Thaman Gurung
Italy, November 1944

Rifleman, Bhanbhagta Gurung
March 1945

Rifleman, Lachhiman Gurung
May 1945

Gurkhas poised for action in Burma

Gurkha recruits of the 2nd Gurkha swear allegiance to their regimental "Truncheon".